The Manager's Guide to
Program Evaluation

Planning, Contracting, and Managing for Useful Results

Paul W. Mattessich, PhD
Wilder Research

With assistance from
Ryan Evans

FIELDSTONE
A L L I A N C E

Fieldstone Alliance
An imprint of Turner Publishing Company, Nashville, Tennessee
www.turnerpublishing.com

Cover design by Grace Cavalier
Book design by Tim Holtz

Library of Congress Cataloging-in-Publication Data
Names: Mattessich, Paul W., author. | Evans, Ryan (Research scientist), contributor.
Title: The manager's guide to program evaluation : planning, contracting, and managing for useful results / Paul W. Mattessich ; with assistance from Ryan Evans.
Description: 2nd edition. | Nashville, Tennessee : Fieldstone Alliance, an imprint of Turner Publishing Company, [2021] | Includes bibliographical references and index.
Identifiers: LCCN 2021026142 (print) | LCCN 2021026143 (ebook) | ISBN 9781684427895 (hardcover) | ISBN 9781684427888 (paperback) | ISBN 9781684427901 (ebook)
Subjects: LCSH: Project management. | Management--Evaluation. | Evaluation. | Evaluation--Methodology.
Classification: LCC HD69.P75 M3784 2021 (print) | LCC HD69.P75 (ebook) | DDC 658.4/04--dc23
LC record available at https://lccn.loc.gov/2021026142
LC ebook record available at https://lccn.loc.gov/2021026143

To learn more about Wilder Research, contact:
Wilder Research
Amherst H. Wilder Foundation
www.wilder.org/wilder-research

Printed in the United States of America

 Printed on recycled paper 10% postconsumer waste

About the Author

PAUL W. MATTESSICH, PhD, is executive director of Wilder Research, which dedicates itself to improving the lives of individuals, families, and communities through applied research. Mattessich has assisted local, national, and international organizations with strategic planning, organizational improvement, and evaluation. He travels regularly to Northern Ireland and the United Kingdom, where he learns from and consults with organizations addressing youth development, community development, and the promotion of peace and acceptance of diversity among groups from divided communities. Mattessich has been involved in applied social research since 1973 and is the author or coauthor of more than three hundred publications and reports, including the recently released third edition of *Collaboration: What Makes It Work.* He has also served on a variety of task forces in government and the nonprofit sectors. He received his PhD in sociology from the University of Minnesota, where he currently serves as an adjunct faculty in the School of Social Work.

Contents

List of Figures and Tables

adjust to provide more of what works well, and you can discontinue or search for alternatives for what does not work well.

- Improve the allocation of resources. Related to the previous benefit, you can use evaluation findings in combination with financial information to direct more resources to more effective activities and fewer resources to less-effective activities. You can also combine evaluation and financial data to calculate the cost/benefit of alternative ways of providing your services.

- Manage and monitor implementation. Having evaluation findings during the early stages in the development of a program enables you to see immediately how well you are reaching potential clients and delivering the intended services. Have you begun implementation fully and with fidelity to the program plan or model? Sometimes, new or expanding programs may achieve only partial implementation, for reasons such as inadequate funding or inadequate time to train staff and change the way they do their work. Having good information on these issues can help in interpreting program outcomes and what they may indicate about program effectiveness. You can make modifications early to increase your speed and/or effectiveness in reaching your goals.

- Retain or increase funding. Having credible evaluation findings increases your stature in the eyes of funders. Programs that can show what they are doing and how it makes a difference in the lives of individuals, families, or communities will, on average, find themselves in a stronger position for funding. (Some of Wilder Research's long-term evaluation clients have reported that they've won grants and contracts—despite heavy competition and shrinking resources—because they base their proposals to private and government funders upon complete, accurate, impartial evaluation findings.)

- Collaborate for community impact. Sometimes, you will collaborate with other organizations, not just to improve the services in each organization but to increase the overall community impact of your total efforts as well.[3] It has become more and more common for organizations to

---

[3]   See an example of agencies working together to improve their overall effectiveness in addressing a shared vision and common goals in Moira Inkelas, et al., "Improvement for a Community Population: The Magnolia Community Initiative." *New Directions for Program Evaluation* 2017:153: 51–64.

seek collective impact. It has also become more common for funders to require collaboration in public health, education, and other community initiatives. Your evaluation can demonstrate to collaborators and funders the value you bring to collective impact partnerships.[4]

Evaluation as an Ongoing Process of Doing and Learning

The Greek word "praxis" connotes doing or action. The word sounds a bit like "practice." Many of us say that we "practice" our profession. In addition, all of our work is "practice" in the sense that we learn from it and constantly strive to do better.

Applied research and evaluation should contribute to praxis and lead to effective action.[5] In our definition of evaluation, we emphasized the words "so that" because the goal of evaluation is action. Evaluation is a tool to help improve the actions taken by your organization. You can use evaluation information to make progress in helping individuals, groups, and communities. People who do program evaluation do not receive their motivation from writing reports but from observing the results of their work being translated into action.

What influences program decision-making?

How does evaluation fit into the process of service design and delivery? How does it inform decisions and lead to action?

Think about how you decide what kinds of programs you should develop or what kinds of services or activities you should offer. What goes into that decision? When I ask this question to groups of managers from nonprofit organizations and government agencies, they usually offer a range of responses stating that they make decisions based on things such as "what we learned about community needs," "what funders expect and will pay

---

[4] See Paul W. Mattessich and Kirsten Johnson. *Collaboration: What Makes It Work* (Turner Publishing Co., 2018). See also, Ann Webb Price, Kyrah K. Brown, and Susan M. Wolfe, "What are Coalitions and Collaboratives?" *New Directions for Program Evaluation.* 2020:165: 9–16.

[5] Someone also once said to me that the word "praxis" sounds a bit like "pray"—something which she and her nonprofit organization colleagues often found the need to do, but that's another story.

for," "what's known to be effective," "what we're trained and competent to provide," "what we're used to," and "what other people are offering."

The following paragraphs categorize the types of influences that affect decision-making among managers who are developing a new program. We describe each category and suggest whether and how these influences should actually play a role in your decision-making.

Research findings

Research findings include knowledge acquired through studies of at least four types:

- Assessments of needs—identifies the service needs or desires among the populations you have an interest in serving

- Inventories of services—descriptions of what services people with needs can already access

- Research related to human behavior (in the social sciences, for example)

- Research related to organizational behavior (also in the social sciences)

Research provides a general understanding of what services might be appropriate for the people you're interested in serving. It can also document who else is providing services and assist you to decide what your specific focus might be. The greater the amount of solid research you have that is relevant to your program, the better.

Program evaluation findings

Program evaluation findings include knowledge provided by studies that explored the effectiveness of programs, services, activities, or treatments that are identical or similar to those under consideration by you. Once you have done your own evaluation, you can of course add your own findings to your collection of relevant program evaluation findings.

In general, you will want to use as much of this information as possible. Program evaluation findings, when available, offer a detailed look at how your program (or a similar program) works and how effective it is. You can find good, web-based resources that inform you of previous evaluation research.[6]

Practice wisdom

Practice wisdom includes knowledge gained by the professionals within your organization and by their peers in other organizations. It comes from the experience of working with the population you want to serve.

The strength of practice wisdom comes from the details it provides that research and program evaluation cannot. The weakness comes from the sometimes narrowly focused perspective that practitioners in a specific organization develop because they only see people and situations of limited types.

Valuable Partners: Practice Wisdom and Evaluation

Practice wisdom is the knowledge gained by and shared among professionals, and others, working in a specific field. Such wisdom is invaluable, and it often leads to many improvements. It provides a deep view typically not available through evaluation.

But practice wisdom has an important weakness: the professionals in a given field often come to share a narrow perspective based on an incomplete picture of their work or field. This is where the information independently provided by evaluation can help program professionals and managers gain a broader perspective than that available to them through first-hand experience alone.

Here's an example. Wilder Research once conducted a survey of 150 staff who worked in organizations that served elderly people.

We asked the staff to describe characteristics of the elderly population in general—not the people they served, but *all* older people. The survey respondents greatly overestimated the percentage of people in the general population who had disabilities, who lacked family support, and who could not achieve activities of daily living. This is understandable, since people form impressions based on their observations, and these staff primarily saw elderly people experiencing a high level of challenges. But their "practice wisdom" was incorrect when applied to all older people, and it would be risky to design new programs for the broader elderly population based on this misperception.

---

6   Resources that offer easy-to-use summaries of existing research, to assist you in shaping your program, include: What Works Clearinghouse https://ies.ed.gov/ncee/wwc/, The Cochrane Collaboration https://www.cochrane.org/, The Campbell Collaboration https://www.campbellcollaboration.org/, and SAMHSA Evidence-Based Practices Resource Center.

Interests of stakeholders

Information, opinions, and other miscellaneous inputs from people with a stake in the success of a program can make a difference in final decisions about programming. For example:

• The wisdom and preferences of community members served by the program.

• The interests of a donor who provided funds for a specific program or building or activity.

• The fact that staff have training and experience in one procedure and not in another.

• Politics of various sorts, along with predominant fads of the times.

These influences have value, but they require careful assessment when making program decisions. For example, if a donor wants to provide funds for something which research and evaluation have documented as very effective—that's all for good. If staff are trained and experienced in best practice techniques, that's good as well. However, you would not implement a program just because someone wants to fund it if, for example, research shows that it cannot produce results.

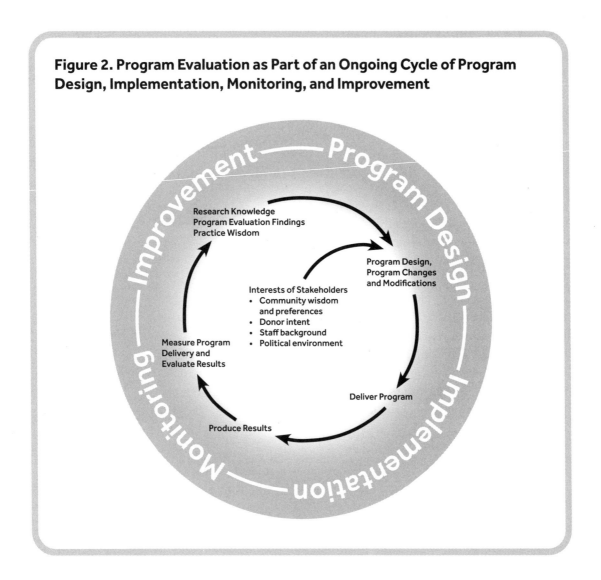

Figure 2. Program Evaluation as Part of an Ongoing Cycle of Program Design, Implementation, Monitoring, and Improvement

Figure 2 illustrates the ongoing cycle of program design, implementation, monitoring, and improvement among program managers and other decision-makers. You use research knowledge, program evaluation findings, practice wisdom, and the interests of stakeholders to shape the design of a program. Then, you deliver or implement the program. This produces results. If you do evaluation, you can complete the cycle by measuring the program's results reliably and adding to your collection of relevant program evaluation findings. Then you can make program changes based on the research, evaluation, and practice wisdom acquired, and continue repeating the cycle—an ongoing process of acting, learning, and improving what you do.

Summary

In this chapter, you have learned what evaluation is: essentially, the formalization of common sense approaches to making decisions. You've learned about the benefits of evaluation and have taken a first look at how you can use it in a process of ongoing improvement. In the next chapter, you will learn about the kinds of information you will need for an evaluation and important questions you can answer with that information.

2

Evaluation Information:
What You Should Have, What It Will Offer You, and How a Good Theory Ties It All Together

Not everything that counts can be counted, and
not everything that can be counted counts.
                    —Anonymous

If you can define it, we can measure it!
                    —Wilder Research

The first statement above is often mistakenly attributed to Albert Einstein. Whoever came up with it should be thanked by both applied researchers and human services practitioners. While no Einstein, the person did have a certain genius for "relativity"—that is, the relative value of information.

The second statement comes from some friendly joking that often occurs among the staff at Wilder Research and the staff in the programs we work with. Although it sometimes appears that science lacks the necessary measurement tools to represent what a program does, in reality that might not be the case. Rather, it might be that we need to clearly define the program's activities and goals. Once that definition occurs, measurement procedures are often quite obvious.

Jointly, these statements usher us into this chapter with two important lessons to keep in mind.

- First, evaluation, similar to all forms of research, has strengths and limitations. Just as in the world of physics, for example, sometimes you suspect that something exists out there, but you can't quite define it, and your measurement tools can't quite detect it. Other times, your measurement tools have taken you as far as you want to go, and the next step is to come up with some new hunches or theories to lead you to further research.

- Second, for evaluation to serve as a tool, you will need to be very clear about what you hope to accomplish. You will need to develop formal definitions of words such as "service," "activity," "client," and "outcomes." You will need to state what your program does, who receives it, and its expected outcomes in clear terms.

In this chapter, we will spend time on two important topics: the types of evaluation information you need and the development of a program theory for your program. Our discussion of evaluation information will enable you to recognize the information you should collect in order to respond to important strategic and operational management questions. It lists four essential types of information with examples for each type. As the word *essential* implies, you must have these four types of information in order to produce a high-quality evaluation.

The discussion of program theory will help you "connect the dots" between the four essential types of information—to combine the evaluation information you have into a portrait of how your services or activities achieve their intended outcomes. A high-quality evaluation can sometimes occur without a program theory. However, the complexity of most programs makes the development of a program theory a requirement for a high-quality evaluation. In addition, many funders mandate the development of logic models (which are a technique for representing a program theory). In those cases, having a program theory becomes a requirement.

The chapter concludes with an overarching perspective that must permeate the selection of information to gather, the decisions about how to gather that information, the interpretation of whatever information you gather, and your construction of a program theory: cultural responsiveness.

Types of Evaluation Information

To understand what your organization or program does and how effective it is—and to obtain ideas on how you might improve your services—your program should strive to include the following types of information in your evaluation efforts, but you may not be able to include all of them in your initial efforts, especially some of the "additional information" items:

Essential information

1. Participant/client information[7]
2. Service data
3. Documentation of results or outcomes[8]
4. Perceptions about your services

Additional information

5. Demographic information on the service area or market area that you serve
6. Data about needs in your community and other communities
7. Comparable measures from organizations similar to yours
8. Financial/cost information
9. Information that identifies the people you serve, such as their name or a unique identification number

---

[7]   Different professions and different service sectors tend to use different terms to refer to the people they serve. In this book, we most frequently refer to "clients"—a common term in human service organizations, among social workers, and in industries where individuals receive a professional service. Terms which other types of organizations commonly use include, for example: patients, participants, patrons, attendees, students, visitors, and members.

[8]   In our discussion, we use the words "results" and "outcomes" to refer to changes that occur, because of the services, treatments, activities, or other efforts of an organization, to the individuals, groups, communities, or organizations that are the recipients of these efforts. Results or outcomes might fall into categories of physical, mental, social, financial, or other.

The Value of Perception

Program managers often want to know what people think of the programs they offer. Some evaluators might argue that such perceptions of a program or service are not an "essential" type of information. In other words, in many cases you could demonstrate effectiveness without understanding whether people actually like a program. Strictly speaking, this is true. However, knowing how people feel about a program has many implications for planning and marketing the program. It also can offer valuable insight into why things work, whether they are likely to continue to work, and how they can be improved.

For example, immunizations protect humans very effectively from serious diseases. However, if few people show up for immunizations because the unpleasant medical experience outweighs the perceived benefits of receiving the immunization, the program will be ineffective. This is a case in which measurement of perception is essential evaluation information; it's essential to change something in the program design, perhaps specifically in its marketing, so that adults will receive immunizations and parents will choose to immunize their children.

Essential evaluation information

You would be surprised at how many organizations don't systematically collect and retain the first two types of information listed above. Many large, well-known, relatively effective organizations find themselves in the situation of having this information only partially.[9] It hampers their ability to evaluate their work and to improve their efforts despite how much they would like to do so.

A description of the four essential types of information listed appears in Figure 3. Note that the examples are literally that: illustrations of typical elements of data that fall into a specific category and that many organizations collect. The specific information that you collect will depend upon your needs and aspirations for the evaluation, your program goals, and your program theory (which we discuss later). The information you choose to collect will also depend on specific hypotheses or questions that you and others have about effectiveness, accessibility, and why things work or don't work.

---

[9] See Paul W. Mattessich, "Lessons Learned: What These Seven Studies Teach Us," *Cancer Practice* 2001:9: 78–84.

Your ability to collect information is tempered by practical considerations, such as what is reasonable to collect and what costs are involved. Do not feel that you must gather all of the information listed in the examples under "typical elements" in order to do a good evaluation.

If you have the information listed in Figure 3, you will possess the basic building blocks to represent your organization's efforts and accomplishments. The information listed there can enable you to respond to a large number of important questions that you and others have in mind when you begin to do a program evaluation. In addition, as new questions arise, you can organize the information in new ways to respond to those questions.

Figure 3. Four Essential Types of Information

Types of evaluation information	Examples of typical elements*
1. *Participant/client information.* That is, information on whom you serve, their characteristics, needs, and other attributes.	• Age, gender, ethnicity, income, education, place of residence, marital status, family status • Interests • Personal abilities • Needs, goals to achieve, problems to resolve • Capacities, resources
2. *Service data.* That is, type, volume, and other features of the services you provide or the activities you offer.	• Type of service or activity provided • Amount of service received (service unit might be a "session," an "hour," an "item," a "dose," an "event") • Extent to which clients/participants complete the program and/or receive the expected services • Staff who offered the service activity (position, demographics, length of experience, or other characteristics)
3. *Documentation of results or outcomes.* That is, evidence of changes that have occurred, accomplishments that have been achieved, or needs that have been met among the people, families, groups, communities, or organizations that you serve.	• Knowledge gained, skills acquired • Problems resolved, needs met • Changes in the status of an individual, family, organization, community, or other group (Changes can occur, for example, in behaviors, physical attributes, feelings, or relationships and patterns of interaction. Monitoring of changes could focus on educational attainment, wages/income, housing, legal, and health status, for example.)
4. *Perceptions about your services.* That is, an indication of how people feel about what you do—in general and about specific aspects of your activities. (Typically, this information comes from users or recipients of your services, but it could also come from non-users.)	• Feelings about the organization or program overall • Ratings of quality of service • Ratings of staff performance (for example, their ability to do their job, to listen and respond to questions) • Ratings of facilities (for example, location, safety, ease of entry, appropriateness of furnishings and decoration for different groups) • Perceptions of accessibility (for example, hours, transportation, and other facilitators and barriers that affect use)

* As we stated earlier, you don't need to collect all of these. They are just examples.

Additional evaluation information

To accomplish the objectives that you have for evaluating your organization, you may need the additional information listed earlier, such as:

5. Demographic information on the service area or market area that you serve

6. Financial/cost information

7. Comparable measures from organizations similar to yours

8. Data about needs in your community and other communities (for example, poverty rates, academic achievement rates, illness incidence or prevalence rates, crime rates, or other social indicators)

9. Information that identifies the people you serve, such as their name or unique identification number

We will discuss why this additional information is important when we look at the types of questions that evaluation information can answer in the next section. You can do a good evaluation without this extra information, but it is required for some questions that you might wish to answer, now or in the future.

Some people will argue that to truly demonstrate effectiveness, comparative data of some sort must enter into an evaluation. That is, comparative data are "essential" not "additional." This argument has some merit. In fact, later on, we discuss the value of providing comparative data for increasing the credibility and usefulness of your evaluation findings. Nonetheless, a program just initiating evaluation can learn a great deal about itself without comparative data, and it should not be discouraged if it cannot obtain such data immediately. Likewise, some people might suggest the necessity of cost data. Organizations often use cost information if they want to study cost benefit or cost effectiveness.

Before exploring items 5–8 above, let's take a moment to discuss item 9, information that identifies the people you serve.

Information that identifies the people you serve

One special type of participant/client information is information that specifically identifies people whom you serve, that is, their names, addresses, Social Security numbers, phone numbers, and other details that can reveal their identity. Some of this you may gather as part of normal record keeping for your organization. Some of it may sit in a database that you use for recording membership, mailing information to people, or other uses. Some of this information may be required to determine a person's eligibility to receive your organization's services. What about its use in program evaluation?

Information that identifies people individually *never* appears in the final report from an evaluation, but it often constitutes an absolutely essential element for the completion of an evaluation study. For example:

- You will need to retain an accurate record of names, addresses, email addresses, and phone numbers if you want to do a follow-up survey of people who used your services in the past (for example, emailing them a questionnaire shortly after they used your services or calling them for an interview a year after they used your services).

- You may need to obtain addresses for an analysis that will identify the places from which you draw people to your organization. (The evaluation jargon for this is *geocode*.)

In order to carry out a program evaluation, you will generally need information that identifies people who use your services or take part in your activities, but it will not become part of the data that go into your findings.

Of course, some evaluation studies, especially those which only assess satisfaction at the time of an event or service episode and for which you have very limited expectations, do not require any information that identifies respondents. For example, a brief survey of persons who attended a presentation or viewed an exhibit can occur completely anonymously. However, you could not return to those participants to assess their satisfaction at a later date or to determine whether they had been able to put to use anything that they learned at the session.

Questions Evaluation Information Can Answer

If you have the information we discussed in the previous sections, you can respond to a number of important management questions, as Figure 4 indicates. For example, you can combine the essential information you've collected about your clients' characteristics with demographic information on your service area to answer the questions, "What proportion of our service area do we reach? Do we seem to reach certain types of people more than others?"

Figure 4 can assist you in a variety of ways. If you are designing an evaluation:

- The figure lets you know what certain types of information can do for you, as well as what information is required for responding to questions that you have.

- It offers a rationale for collecting information. You may need this rationale to justify an expenditure of time or money to collect certain information.

- It suggests evaluation questions for you to include in your design.

- It helps you communicate with a consultant about what you want and why you want it.

If you already have some information about your organization, the people you serve, and the services you provide:

- The figure suggests questions that you may want to consider asking.

- It enables you to determine, by means of the rows and columns, the questions that can be answered with the information currently at your disposal—either just using the information you have or in combination with other information.

Figure 4. Questions Evaluation Information Can Answer

Types of information	Questions you can answer with this information	Additional questions you can answer if you also have other information
Participant/client information. That is, information on whom you serve, their characteristics, needs, and other attributes.	• What kinds of people do we serve? • How many do we serve? • What are their needs? • Where do they come from? • Are these the people we have the mission or intention to serve? • Have we reached the goals we have for amount and types of persons served? • Do certain types of people have needs that differ from those of other types of people? • Do we see certain patterns in who we serve from year to year? • How are client characteristics, needs, or other attributes of the people we serve changing over time? • How well do characteristics of staff match characteristics of the people we serve? • Does our program deliver services as fully as intended and with fidelity to the program plan or model? Are quality standards met for initial assessment of clients/participants, developing client/participant service plans, and delivery of the services?	*With demographic information on your service area or market area, you can also answer:* • What proportion of the people in our service/market area do we reach? • Do we seem to reach certain types of people more than others? • Do changes in the people we serve reflect changes in the service/market area? • What do the demographics and physical location of the people we serve suggest about our accessibility? Do we seem more accessible to some groups than to others? • Can we predict likely changes in the area we serve that we need to plan for? *With cost information:* • What is our cost per person? • Does cost differ for different types of people? *With information from similar programs:* • How do we compare to our peer organizations in number and types of persons served? • Are other organizations experiencing the same changes as we? If so, has this occurred during the same time period? *With information on comparable geographic areas:* • Are the changes we see in our area similar to or different from those in other areas? • Can we predict from the experience of other areas things that we need to anticipate in our area to meet the population's needs?

The list of questions in column 2 and column 3 provides examples. It is not an exhaustive list of the questions that can be answered by the information in column 1.

Figure 4. Questions Evaluation Information Can Answer (continued)

Types of information	Questions you can answer with this information	Additional questions you can answer if you also have other information
Service data. That is, type, volume, and other features of the services you provide or the activities you offer, plus staffing data.	• What services do people receive from our organization? What activities do they take part in? • How much do they receive or take part in? For how long? • Do certain types of people differ from others in what they receive, or in the amount they receive, or in the length of time they use our services or activities?* • Have we reached the goals we have for service? • How much service or activity do staff provide? What is the ratio of staff to service? • Do certain types of staff focus on, or limit themselves to, working with certain types of people we serve? • Do certain types of staff provide more or less service than others? • How are services or activities changing over time?	*With demographic information on your service area or market area, you can also answer:* • How do service area characteristics relate to the services or activities we actually deliver? Are our services or activities aligned with the likely needs or desires of people in our service area? • Can we predict likely changes in the area we serve that we need to plan for? How might we plan for service or activity changes based on these predictions? *With cost information:* • What is our cost per unit of service, per staff person? • Does cost per service unit differ for different types of people who receive our services, or for different types of staff? *With information from similar programs:* • How do we compare to our peer organizations with respect to service type and volume? How do we compare on cost per service unit, per staff person? • Have services or activities in other organizations exhibited the same changes as ours? If so, has this occurred during the same time period? *With information on comparable geographic areas:* • Are the changes we see in our area similar or different to those in other areas? How might we plan for service or activity changes based on changes in these other areas? • Do service delivery trends in other areas have implications for the way we should think about providing service?

*   Questions such as these in column 2 assume that you have information available from other parts of the figure. For example, to answer this question, you need both service data (from this part of the figure) and client/participant characteristics data (from the previous part of the figure).

Figure 4. Questions Evaluation Information Can Answer (continued)

Types of information	Questions you can answer with this information	Additional questions you can answer if you also have other information
Documentation of results or outcomes. That is, evidence of changes that have occurred, accomplishments that have been achieved, or needs that have been met among the people, organizations, and/or communities that you serve.	• Do we meet the needs that people bring to us? • What impacts do we have on the people we serve, or on organizations or communities? • Does this differ for different types of people who receive our services?* • Have we reached the goals we have for effectiveness? • How have our results been changing over time? • How is the volume of service people receive related to impact or effectiveness?	*With demographic information on your service area or market area, you can also answer:* • Does anything special exist in our area that might enhance or limit how effective we can be? • Do the characteristics of those who experience positive impact from our work match the characteristics of the people we most want to reach in our area? *With cost information:* • What does it cost to produce a successful "result"? • Does the cost of a successful result differ for different types of people who receive our services, or for different types of staff, or for different regions of our service area? *With information from similar programs:* • How do we compare to our peer organizations with respect to successful results or outcomes? • Do other organizations have the same kinds of results that we do? If so, has this occurred during the same time period? *With information on comparable geographic areas:* • Do similar organizations in other areas produce similar results or outcomes? What are the implications of this for us?

---

* This question has special importance for culturally responsive evaluation of programs serving varied cultures.

All of this, of course, enables you to improve your programs and do a better job fulfilling the mission that your organization has.[12]

Before we move to discuss logic models, take note that the use of the term "engineer" does not imply that only someone with professional training can connect the dots to explain why a program produces the outcomes it produces. Anyone can observe information, systematically interpret that information based on their education or lived experience, draw conclusions, and construct a theory.

A way to represent program theories: Logic models

Logic models offer a method to portray your program's theory. One format for logic models that has become popular includes four components: inputs, activities, outputs, and outcomes. Outcomes are sometimes subdivided into initial outcomes, intermediate outcomes, and longer-term outcomes.[13] Figure 5 describes these components.

---

[12] For a good, brief discussion of program theories and evaluation, see Patricia J. Rogers, Anthony Petrosino, Tracy A. Huebner, and Timothy A. Hacsi, "Program Theory Evaluation: Practice, Promise, and Problems" in *Program Theory and Evaluation: Challenges and Opportunities*, edited by Patricia J. Rogers, Timothy A. Hacsi, Anthony Petrosino, and Tracy A. Huebner, 5–13 (San Francisco: Jossey-Bass, 2000).

[13] This style of logic models was popularized by United Way of America, *Measuring Program Outcomes: A Practical Approach* (Alexandria, VA: United Way of America, 1996). Other formats for logic models and other ways to represent program theories have appeared over the years. They all constitute variants on a common theme in which a graphic, usually boxes and arrows, portrays a series of steps leading from what a program does to what the program is expected to accomplish. The different formats sometimes use different terms to refer to the same concepts. Most program managers find the United Way's format relatively easy to use. It has evolved over the past quarter century, and it is popular with most large, grantmaking foundations.

Figure 5. Logic Model

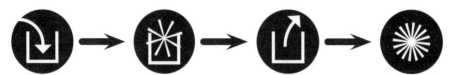

Inputs	Activities	Outputs	Outcomes
Resources a program uses to carry out its activities. For example, staff, supplies, volunteers, money.	The actual work, or services, of a program. Things that staff and volunteers do, such as counseling, training, delivering meals, and other service delivery activities.	The accomplishments, products, or service units of a program. For example, the number of persons who received training.	Changes that occur in people, policies, or something else as a result of a program's activities.

Initial: Changes that a program immediately produces in participants. For example, through training, a program might change people's knowledge, skills, or attitudes.

Intermediate: Changes that occur later as a result of the initial outcomes. For example, people get better paying and more satisfying jobs as a result of knowledge and skills they gained.

Longer Term: Changes that a program ultimately strives to accomplish and that follow from the intermediate outcomes. For example, better paying jobs enable people to maintain a stable income and reside in decent housing.

Figure 6 provides examples of two logic models—one for a teen smoking reduction program, the other for a job skills program. You may want to look at them to assist you in developing a logic model for your program.

Note that you do not have to gather information about everything that appears in the logic model. However, the model can alert you to information that is important to obtain in order to understand the effectiveness of your work.

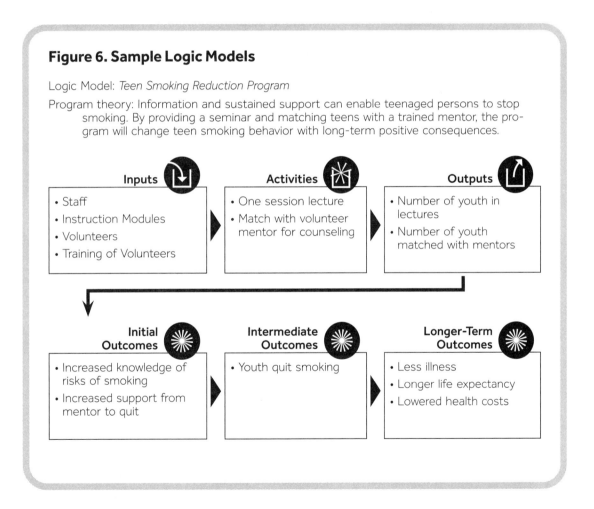

Figure 6. Sample Logic Models

Logic Model: *Teen Smoking Reduction Program*

Program theory: Information and sustained support can enable teenaged persons to stop smoking. By providing a seminar and matching teens with a trained mentor, the program will change teen smoking behavior with long-term positive consequences.

Inputs
- Staff
- Instruction Modules
- Volunteers
- Training of Volunteers

Activities
- One session lecture
- Match with volunteer mentor for counseling

Outputs
- Number of youth in lectures
- Number of youth matched with mentors

Initial Outcomes
- Increased knowledge of risks of smoking
- Increased support from mentor to quit

Intermediate Outcomes
- Youth quit smoking

Longer-Term Outcomes
- Less illness
- Longer life expectancy
- Lowered health costs

Figure 6. Sample Logic Models (continued)

Logic Model: *Job Skills for Unemployed Adults*

Program theory: Improved understanding of employer expectations, along with good job skills and a supervised placement, will lead to stable employment and reduction of welfare use.

Inputs	Activities	Outputs
• Staff • Funding • Buildings/Classrooms	• Classroom instruction • Job placement • Counseling on the job	• Number of adults trained, who are parents • Number of placements • Counseling sessions

Initial Outcomes	Intermediate Outcomes	Longer-Term Outcomes
• Improved understanding of employer expectations • Acquire job skills • Obtain placements	• Secure permanent employment • Have stable income	• Reduce welfare use • Improved economic position of children

Now that we have discussed program theories and have seen a format for representing them, let's return to the assertion that program theories transform us into "engineers" who can understand why something works, can communicate that to others, and can use the knowledge gained from the theory to tackle new and related problems. Reflect on each of these in turn:

Understanding why something works

Consider the case of the job skills program in Figure 6. The theory represented by the logic model expresses how a set of three activities (classroom instruction, job placement, and counseling) ultimately leads to a significant social change (reduction of welfare use). This might seem trivial, but it is certainly not. To illustrate why, imagine two communities, each of which separately initiates a job skills program. The only difference between the two is that Community A has no program theory, while Community B does have a program theory.

In both communities, the number of people on welfare declines only very slightly after the first year of program operation. Due to the expense of the program, public officials and the public at large have become very skeptical and demand that either outcomes improve or the program should discontinue.

Community A, without a program theory—and without any understanding of the dynamics of reducing welfare dependency through job skills train-ing—has no options other than to stay the course or to stop the program (and then to do nothing or try a different program). If you disagree with this, try to explain what else Community A can do, without using terms similar to those in the boxes labeled Outputs, Initial Outcomes, and Inter-mediate Outcomes.

Community B, on the other hand, has more options. For instance, it can reflect on the Initial Outcomes section of its program theory and measure how well program participants did on improving work attitudes, acquiring job skills, and obtaining placements. Assume that Community B discovers that participants who accomplish all three leave welfare, whereas those who accomplish only one or two do not leave welfare. Community B can then change its activities to increase the likelihood that participants will accomplish all three Initial Outcomes.

The reason why Community B could take steps to improve its effectiveness, while Community A could not, is that Community B had something—a program theory—that enabled it to understand how and why the job skills program leads to the intended outcomes.

Communication to others

Logic models are visual and communicate quickly. Note how easily and succinctly the teen smoking and job skills program logic models informed you of what the program does, what it ultimately hopes to accomplish, and everything that logically occurs in between. In the previous example, think how many more ways Community B's program will have to defend itself against cutbacks, while Community A's program is virtually defenseless.

Using knowledge gained from theory to tackle new and related problems

Consider the teen smoking reduction program in Figure 6. Based on the program theory, one can ask whether a program that increases knowledge and provides ongoing support might help in addressing other problems. For example, perhaps the same type of activities might help to reduce drug or alcohol abuse among teens or other age groups.

Cultural Responsiveness

All evaluation research must take cultural context into account. Culture strongly influences how we see the world. It provides values and norms that guide behavior. It offers meaning to specific experiences that we have in life. Language, a part of culture, defines the ways we think, and it offers the primary means that we use to communicate concepts and to express our feelings to other people.

In some evaluation situations, culture seems easy to take for granted. For example, if the people who deliver a program's services share a culture identical to the culture of the recipients of those services, cultural context might seem invisible. Add to that an evaluation researcher who also shares the same culture, and one could think that culture is irrelevant. However, even in such a homogenous arrangement, failure to recognize the importance of culture might lead to faulty research findings.

Contemporary life has less and less homogeneity in modern times. Organizations serving the community typically include a variety of cultures among staff, service recipients, funders, and other stakeholders. Government agencies, along with nongovernmental organizations collaborating with them, have the responsibility to create, deliver, and evaluate services that meet the needs of multiple cultural groups.

Therefore, culturally responsive thought and action in evaluation becomes extremely important.

An early definition of culturally responsive evaluation indicates that "an evaluation is culturally responsive if it fully takes into account the culture of the program that is being evaluated. In other words, the evaluation is based on an examination of impacts through lenses in which the culture of the participants is considered an important factor…"[14]

A more recent essay on culturally responsive evaluation states that it "involves being attuned and responsive to not only the program itself but also to its larger cultural context and the lives and experiences of program staff and stakeholders."[15]

So, what are some important considerations for you? I suggest three things to keep in mind as you work with an evaluator on an evaluation of your program.

First, acknowledge that your own culture will affect the way you approach program evaluation. For example, culture can affect your decisions about the information that you will collect. You will want to reduce the chances that your values, assumptions, and beliefs will create blind spots that might skew the evaluation in the wrong direction. Therefore, request input in whatever way you can to build appropriate cultural understanding into the design of the evaluation, as well as the methods for collecting and inter-preting information that is gathered. We discuss evaluation stakeholders in the next chapter. You will find it valuable to enlist their help in this regard.

Second, include information suggested earlier in this chapter, which rep-resents important dimensions of culture—e.g., demographic characteristics of people you serve and of staff.

---

[14] Veronica Thomas, Henry Frierson, Stafford Hood, and Gerunda Hughes, "A Guide to Conduct-ing Culturally Responsive Evaluations." 75–96 in Frechtling, Joy, *The 2010 User-Friendly Hand-book for Program Evaluation*. (2010, Directorate for Education and Human Resources, National Science Foundation). Also, the Center for Advancement of Informal Science Education provides on its website, funded by the National Science Foundation, a set of contemporary resources for culturally responsive evaluation: https://www.informalscience.org/evaluation/developing -evaluation-plan/resources-culturally-responsive-evaluation

[15] Michelle Bryan and Ashlee Lewis, "Culturally Responsive Evaluation as a Form of Critical Qual-itative Inquiry," *Oxford Research Encyclopedias*, online (2019) https://oxfordre.com/education /view/10.1093/acrefore/9780190264093.001.0001/acrefore-9780190264093-e-545

Third, make sure that you understand the meaning of the information you gather from the cultural perspectives of everyone involved with your program. For example, measuring the percentage of people who have a household income below the poverty level offers quantitative description of purchasing power and access to certain types of resources. The economic implications of poverty might be relatively uniform across cultures. However, the symbolic and psychological significance of a poverty-level income might vary greatly across cultures. Without understanding that, any conclusions you draw based on your measurements could fail to provide you with a sound basis for making improvements in your program.

Summary

This chapter has described the essential information you need for an evaluation of a program as well as other information that can help to provide a portrait of what a program accomplishes. It indicated how you can use different types of information, alone or in combination, to respond to important management questions for your organization or program. The chapter discussed the value of having a program theory to tie together information about your program and to empower you to make wise modifications, improve your effectiveness, and apply your knowledge to a wide array of important issues. Finally, it emphasized the importance of recognizing culture and designing evaluations to be culturally responsive.

Your next question might be: "So, how do we do what needs to be done?" In the next chapter, we will discuss the steps to take to design and implement a program evaluation, highlighting your roles and those of the evaluation researcher.

3

Phases of an Evaluation Study

All research studies, including program evaluation studies, go through the following phases:

• Design

• Data Collection

• Analysis

• Reporting

In this chapter, we will discuss these phases and point to the important details of "who does what" in each phase. The chapter identifies your roles and the researcher's roles. The researcher (or evaluator) is the person who carries out the technical parts of the evaluation study. The researcher can be a consultant you hire, someone on your staff, or you yourself.

No matter who does the work, you, as a program manager, will want to assess whether the evaluator has designed a thorough study. You will want to recognize, anticipate, and discuss potential costs. You will also want to think about the roles of you and your staff in the study, in addition to those of the evaluator. Therefore, this chapter offers an overview of the four phases of a study, along with information about what happens in each phase.

Figure 7 describes the major steps associated with each phase of an evaluation research study.

Figure 7. Program Evaluation Phases and Steps

Phase of Study	Steps in Each Phase*
Design	1. State the program goals, research questions, and other important expectations for the evaluation. 2. Specify your program theory, as appropriate; finalize program goals and evaluation questions. 3. Select appropriate research methods. 4. Finalize estimates of costs, agreements on roles, and plans for activities. 5. Finalize and test methods. 6. Train staff and implement the evaluation.
Data Collection	1. Obtain necessary information using methods developed during the design phase. 2. Clean data. 3. Compile and store data.
Analysis	1. Conduct initial analysis. 2. Review and finalize the analysis.
Reporting	1. Present findings to intended audiences in both oral and written forms. 2. Make other presentations as needed.

* Use of the word "steps" may imply a linear, sequential process. However, the research process is not always linear. Sometimes, after reaching a particular step, a project may move back a step or two, based on new learning or a change in thinking. Also, if you do ongoing evaluation of your program, that is, if you gather information continuously and indefinitely in order to improve your work, then you will repeat the cycle of steps on a regular basis.

In this chapter, we discuss the roles of the researcher and your roles related to each of the steps listed above. (If you plan to do the evaluation research yourself, then the "roles of the researcher" listed in this chapter will also be your roles.) Program managers and evaluation researchers often have different perspectives on an organization's capacity for evaluation (e.g., different opinions about how to collect data) and on evaluation practice (e.g., how results are used) in an organization. In this book, we hope to bring the perceptions and expectations of these two groups closer, in order to promote useful program evaluation.[16]

---

[16] See Leslie A. Fierro and Christina A. Christie, "Evaluator and Program Manager Perceptions of Evaluation Capacity and Evaluation Practice." *American Journal of Evaluation.* 2017:38(3): 376–392.

Design Phase

The adage from the strategic planning literature that "failure to plan is planning to fail" applies with equal weight to the field of evaluation. The design phase, in my opinion, is the single most important stage in your work. Decisions in this phase affect all later steps. Mistakes in this phase may limit, or even completely eliminate, your ability to produce useful evaluation findings.

Sadly, many people, even professional evaluators, sometimes do not devote adequate attention to this phase. They suffer the consequences.

Six steps make up the design phase:

Design Step 1: State the program goals, research questions, and other important expectations for the evaluation.

Design Step 2: Specify your program theory, as appropriate; finalize program goals and evaluation questions.

Design Step 3: Select appropriate research methods.

Design Step 4: Finalize estimates of costs, agreements on roles, and plans for activities.

Design Step 5: Finalize and test methods.

Design Step 6: Train staff and implement evaluation.

You should understand what these steps accomplish and why you need to take them. Then, you can work with an evaluation researcher to structure your own approach.

Keep in mind that not all evaluation work occurs in a neat and tidy manner. You might need to go back and redo one or more steps if you run into something unexpected, for example. Don't worry about that. Nevertheless, in one way or another, you will need to accomplish the activities described in this chapter.

Design
Step 1 ➲

State the program goals, evaluation questions, and other important expectations for the evaluation

In this step, you determine in general what you want the evaluation to do for you. Assuming that you want to measure whether the program accomplishes the goals it has, you will need to state those goals explicitly. For example, your program might have goals such as these:

- To enable unemployed people under age twenty-five to obtain stable employment.

- To improve the graduation rate within a school district.

- To increase the knowledge of children about contemporary painters and sculptors.

- To increase the amount of contact between older people and youth in the community.

- To improve the health of users of the community health clinic.

You and the evaluator will likely discuss what these goals mean, and perhaps even revise them, until you feel comfortable that you have stated something that is worth measuring.

During this step, the specific questions that the evaluation will answer often emerge from asking your stakeholders what they want to learn about the effectiveness of your program or organization. Stakeholders can include anyone who will make a decision based on the evaluation or who will somehow be affected by the results of the evaluation, for example: managers and staff in your organization, funding agencies, and clients. You don't need to involve all possible stakeholders, but you should identify the "primary intended users" of the evaluation and make certain to solicit their input.

Based on your thinking and with input from your stakeholders, you might develop questions such as:

- How many people do we serve in our program?

- With what percentage of people do we actually achieve our goals?

- Are we more successful with some types of people than we are with others?

- What do service recipients feel we need to do to improve?

It is very important to pose questions appropriate for the maturity level of the program. For example, if your program is brand new, and you know you will make many changes in it based on the first year or two of experience, you should probably frame most, even all, of your questions with respect to the program's activities (for example, is the program being delivered as intended?) and program outputs (for example, how many participants are completing the program?). Wait until a later year to attempt to do a study of outcomes.[17] At any time, of course, you can measure the satisfaction of program participants with the services or activities provided, and you can request their suggestions for improvement.

During this step, you also need to state other major expectations. These include:

- Expectations related to cost. You and the evaluation researcher will not reach a final agreement on costs until Design Step 4. However, at the out-set, you should indicate any expectations you have, for example, a "ball-park" range or a maximum budget (if one has been established). As part of this, you might want to develop expectations for the amount of your program's staff time you are willing to allocate to the evaluation work.

- Expectations related to timing. If you feel that the evaluation should produce findings within a certain timeframe, you should state that. If you have deadlines for making decisions, or if you do organizational planning on a cycle that makes it desirable to receive information at a certain time of the year, you should inform the evaluator.

- Expectations concerning communication with the participants in your program. Some evaluation information comes from clients. Do you have expectations as to how or when clients can be asked to provide this

---

[17] Some evaluation texts refer to this as the distinction between a *process evaluation* (looking at activities, services, staff, and organizational features of your operations to document the history and to see whether you deliver what you intend to deliver to the intended consumers) and an *outcome evaluation* (determining whether your program effectively produces the initial, intermediate, and longer-term impacts desired). Problems can result if you attempt to ask questions inappropriate for a program's level of development.

information? Do you have expectations regarding what can, or cannot, be asked? Do you have expectations regarding languages to be used in the collection of information? Do you have expectations regarding confidentiality of information? If so, you should state these.

- Other expectations. You should state anything else you consider important regarding your preferences for the evaluation.

In this step, you do not make absolutely final decisions. Everything—goals, research questions, study methods, costs, and whatever else you consider important—is open for later negotiation and adjustment. However, you should strive to provide as firm an idea of your expectations as possible—so that you, the evaluation researcher, your staff, and others do not expend effort only to be frustrated later when you realize that the work is not moving in an acceptable direction.

Roles of the researcher:

- Work with you to state program goals and identify intended users and other important stakeholders for the evaluation findings.

- Lead a process to identify the evaluation questions to address.

Your roles:

- Identify intended users and other important stakeholders for the evaluation findings.

- Bring those people together, or set up a process that makes sure they have representation in the design. (This may include creating a "committee" of some sort to oversee the work.)

- Express your program goals, state questions you want the evaluation research to answer, and state any other expectations you have for the work.

How this step usually occurs:

Some of this work often begins even before you have met with the evaluation researcher who will collaborate with you. For example, you may have already formulated your goals and the research questions you want answered. You may already have some general cost limits or some guide-lines related to how your program's clients or participants can be involved in the evaluation.

However, much of the work occurs through interaction between you and the evaluator in meetings, written correspondence, and phone calls.

Most commonly, activities in this step include:

- Several meetings between you and the evaluator.

- A preliminary letter of understanding in which the evaluator states tenta-tively what the evaluation will accomplish, how it will occur, and what it might cost.

- A meeting of your advisory committee to discuss what the evaluator proposes.[18]

Specify your program theory, as appropriate; finalize program goals and evaluation questions

Design
Step 2

This step is crucial whether or not you plan to do an evaluation that mea-sures the outcomes of your program.[19] Your immediate plan may just be to gather information on whom you are serving, what they receive from you, and how satisfied they are. However, eventually, you will need to measure outcomes. Your initial evaluation should be designed with this possibility in mind.

Roles of the researcher:

- Collaborate with you to finalize program goals in language that makes clear how you define effectiveness; finalize evaluation questions.

- Collaborate with you to develop your program theory.

---

[18] For tips on effective use of an advisory committee in contract and grant-funded research, see Paul W. Mattessich, "Advisory Committees in Contract and Grant-Funded Research." *New Directions in Evaluation* 2012:136: 31–48.

[19] That is, an evaluation that gathers information of the third type, in the model we examined in the previous chapter. See Figure 3.

Your roles:

- Finalize program goals in clear, measurable terms; collaborate in finalizing evaluation questions.

- Develop a program theory/logic model.

How this step usually occurs:

Most commonly, activities in this step include:

- One or more meetings between you and the evaluator. (These meetings, of course, may be the same meetings at which you accomplish the work outlined in the previous step.)

- Reviewing program goals and evaluation questions that you and other stakeholders for the evaluation modify and reach consensus about, with the evaluator.

- Drafting a program theory or logic model (by you or the evaluation researcher) for review, revision, and consensus among you and other stakeholders for the evaluation.

Design
Step 3 ➲

Select appropriate research methods

Whoever does the research should take the lead in this step. By now, the evaluation researcher should have developed a good understanding of what you want to accomplish. Also, they should have reviewed and considered alternative approaches to evaluation that have been used for programs similar or identical to yours.

You will address the questions: What's the right method? How should we gather information? Remember that evaluation is just an extension of common sense. You know from common sense that no matter what you want to do—cure an illness, repair your car, have a pleasant vacation—a variety of methods exist. You will pick the one that best suits you at a particular time. You'll have certain priorities, and you will judge each potential method in terms of those priorities.

Similarly, with evaluation, a variety of methods exist. Not all of them are right in all circumstances. In addition, some might fit at one point in the development of a program, but not fit at another point. You and the evaluator will want to make sure that you match the method you use to the needs you have.

Warning: Be skeptical about any evaluator who jumps to a recommendation about research methods before fully understanding what you need to know and how you plan to use the findings of the evaluation research. For example, evaluators who strongly suggest "surveys" or "focus groups" very early in the conversation, or who emphasize that they always use "experimental design" or "qualitative methods," probably won't provide you the service you need. You should first identify what information you need, at what level of precision, in what format—and *then* work backwards to the appropriate method for obtaining that information.

Figure 8 shows a few typical methods for gathering information for an evaluation, along with examples of reasons why you and an evaluation researcher might select them.

Figure 8. Typical Information-Gathering Methods

Method	Reason for use
Use of your program's records (Can provide "Essential information" types 1, 2, 3 in Figure 3 of Chapter 2)	Commonly, forms completed by service recipients or staff offer the best source of information on the demographics of service recipients, their reasons for applying to participate in the program or to receive a service, and other characteristics of service recipients that you will need for your evaluation. In addition, records documenting services received, attendance, program completion, or other activities will typically provide the information you require to understand which services clients receive, who participates in events, and other happenings in your program. Assessment records in your program can document changes in the physical, mental, social, and economic conditions of service recipients. That information indicates outcomes of your program. Unique identifiers—a name, address, ID number, or something similar—for each service recipient enables you to tie information together across different records and different databases. It is essential if, for example, you want to gather information at different time points—e.g., at the time people start and complete a program—in order to determine whether the services they received produced the intended effects. Staffing records provide information on the social characteristics, educational and professional backgrounds, and experience of staff. That information can help you to describe how you provide service; it enables you to assess the match between your workforce and the needs you want to meet among your clients and within the community you serve; and it enables you to understand whether differences in process or outcome exist between different types of staff. Financial records enable you to explore the cost effectiveness of your services and to test means for providing effective service at the lowest cost.
Surveys: Service recipients and persons associated with service recipients (for example, family members) (Can provide "Essential information" types 3, 4 in Figure 3 of Chapter 2)	Telephone surveys, mail surveys, web surveys, and in-person surveys offer a way to obtain information on what your program means for people and what impacts it has in their lives. In most cases, service recipients themselves will participate. In some cases, family members might provide information on behalf of, or to supplement, information received by service recipients (e.g., children). Surveys, if the samples are large enough and representative, can provide sound information on how well the program achieves its goals, what perceptions people hold about the program, and other matters. However, depending on how you do a survey and on the ability of respondents to provide detailed explanations, a survey might not obtain the depth of information that you would like to obtain.

Figure 8. Typical Information-Gathering Methods (continued)

Method	Reason for use
Focus groups: Service recipients, staff, other people with knowledge relevant to your research questions (Can provide "Essential information" types 3, 4 in Figure 3 of Chapter 2)	Focus groups can serve as a good means for obtaining information if you don't need a systematically drawn, large sample as the basis for drawing conclusions. Focus groups typically involve eight to twelve people with similar experiences with your program, such as service recipients or staff. Especially in the developmental stages of a program, focus groups can generate advice and suggestions for program improvement. Over time, they can play a similar role discussing issues that arise and making recommendations to address issues or improve the program. To some extent, you can learn about people's perceptions of the program. But the value of this information is tempered by the lack of confidentiality, "group think" dynamics, the unwillingness of some people who may have strong opinions to attend a focus group, and the possibility that the group(s) is not representative of the population you seek information from.
Observation by a researcher (Can provide "Essential information" types 2, 3 in Figure 3 of Chapter 2)	The measurement of some program achievements may require having a neutral party make observations, for example, to record behavior during a meeting or during a classroom instruction session. Such observation may also be useful in determining whether a program is being delivered as intended.
Assessments by staff (Can provide "Essential information" type 3 in Figure 3 of Chapter 2)	Measurement of progress or outcomes for service recipients may sometimes require a professional assessment by someone acquainted with them. In this case, members of your staff may complete assessment forms.

Figure 8. Typical Information-Gathering Methods (continued)

Method	Reason for use
Use of databases ("big data") (Can provide "Essential information" types 1, 2, 3 in Figure 3 of Chapter 2)	Useful data often exist in databases maintained by government agencies, academic institutions, large health care deliverers and insurers, and similar organizations. If you have access to this type of information, you can use it to develop indicators related to the people you serve (your clients, patients, or patrons). You can also use it to develop baselines and comparisons helpful for you in assessing the effectiveness of services you provide to the individuals you serve. Such comparative data might also be available from programs/organizations similar to yours. If your program has the mission to produce change in an entire community, then existing databases may contain all the information you need to take a before-during-after look which documents the impacts of your work on that community. Existing databases (sometimes called "big data") include US Census information, which can be helpful in understanding the demographic characteristics of your service area or market area. Other existing databases include records from government agencies (e.g., unemployment data, educational attainment data, hospitalization rates, and crime information), telecommunication and social media data, and others. Sometimes you can obtain information from these databases that directly links to the people you serve; sometimes you can only obtain aggregate information for a geographic area which can be helpful in understanding the needs in your community or other communities.[*] Sometimes, you will be able to obtain aggregate information about a group of people who received your services, or about the people in a specific geographic area. Sometimes, you will be able to obtain information about specific individuals your organization served.

[*] Robert Picciotto, "Evaluation and the Big Data Challenge." *American Journal of Evaluation.* 2020:41(2): 166–181 notes that "Big Data holds enormous promise for extending the reach and improving the quality of evaluation practice." (166) But he also points out that it has increased information overload and introduced new threats such as inaccurate algorithmic predictions, automated decision-making, and faulty modeling.

Roles of the researcher:

- Select methods of data collection that will meet the research goals.

- Draft a statement of methods that the evaluation will use. Discuss it with you, and revise it.

- Draft a statement that clarifies responsibilities for collection of information. Discuss it with you, and revise it.

- Initiate necessary research review and approval processes. These may include *human subjects review*, if required[20], approvals or purchases of research instruments from license holders or vendors, and other approvals as needed.

Your roles:

- React to the suggestions of the researcher. Give your opinions on the proposed methods.

- Accept tentatively, or reject, the researcher's suggestions regarding responsibilities for collection of information.

- Instigate any other review processes that your organization, funders, regulators, and other stakeholders may require.

How this step usually occurs:

- The researcher will probably spend time outside of meetings with you thinking about the best methods to respond to the study questions. The researcher will communicate with you about these methods via meetings, phone calls, and written correspondence.

- During the design phase, often at about this step, a good researcher will suggest some potential findings and ask you: "If this is what you learned, would it enable you to do what you need to do?" Your response will either confirm that the design matches your needs, or it will indicate that the design requires adjustment.

---

[20] Most government-funded research, and most research carried out by academic institutions, must pass *human subjects review* prior to the collection of any study data (even for method testing). A committee (the *human subjects committee*) must review the research design to assess informed consent, confidentiality, and risk to the participants in the research. Federal regulations, sometimes referred to as the Common Rule, specify necessary protections for persons involved in research studies. Note, though, that most program evaluation research does not require review by a human subjects committee.

Design
Step 4 ➜

Finalize estimates of costs, agreements on roles, and plans for activities

This step finalizes the overall design. After this step, everyone should be clear about what the evaluation will do, how it will occur, and what it will cost.

That being said, some projects move beyond this step with only a general understanding and then revisit it. Several situations can produce the need to amend your "final" estimates of costs, agreement on roles, or plans for activities related to the evaluation. For example, the following situations will affect costs:

• Sometimes in finalizing your methods, you learn something that indicates you will need more time or more resources. Or you learn that a particular method will not work as planned, and you need to select another method. Sometimes you find out that information you assumed already existed actually does not exist.[21] Sometimes as the evaluation progresses, you identify additional information that you want or need. This often requires more time or other resources. Sometimes, you discover that an initially established timeline for obtaining information no longer works, and you need to expand or delay some evaluation tasks.

At about this point in the process, many programs find it helpful to develop a written document to make certain that everyone understands their responsibilities. In a few pages, this document can lay out the way the evaluation work will proceed. Figure 9 shows the typical contents of such a document.

---

[21] This happens very frequently in organizations that have developed record systems to gather information but have not made use of the information and have not maintained a quality control process for the information. They typically learn that the database they assumed, early in the design, that they could use actually has a severe lack of complete and accurate information. Always check if data are complete and accurate.

Figure 9. Typical Evaluation Agreement

Outline section	Content
Name of the program	Whatever people normally call the program. If the focus of the evaluation is not the entire program, but some activities or services, or project within the program, that should be named.
Overview of the program	A paragraph that describes what the program does, who it serves, where it is located, and other key features that provide important context to someone who consults the document.
Activities or services provided	A list of the activities or services of the program, along with a brief notation of what each activity or service entails.
Program theory and logic model	A description and visual diagram, if possible, of how the inputs and activities of the program logically relate to outputs and intended outcomes.
List of program goals	A clear statement of each goal in simple, measurable terms.
Measurement or indicator(s) for each evaluation question	A description of the way that each goal will be measured. In many cases this can just be a reference to some items on a questionnaire, or to some information extracted from a form.
The procedures used to collect the information for each measurement or indicator	The "who, what, when, and where" of how to obtain needed data or information for the evaluation. For each measurement, there should be a description of who gathers the information, using what instrument, and at what time. For example, "A program assistant will complete the exit interview with each participant within the week prior to graduation."
Persons responsible	Anyone with responsibility for any part of the evaluation work should be identified, along with a list of their roles and duties.
List of data collection forms	All forms (program records, survey instruments, other forms or instruments) used for collection of information for the evaluation should be listed, and copies should be attached to the document.

Role of the researcher:

- Prepare a final design, including adequate details on methods, responsibilities of all persons involved, and costs.

Your roles:

- Ask in-depth questions to make sure the researcher has developed the design in a way that will meet your needs.

- Review and come to agreement on the final details.

- Commit necessary resources.

How this step usually occurs:

- This step should include a written document, contract, or statement to which everyone agrees.

- Activities during this step typically include meetings, phone conversations, emails, and postal mail correspondence.

- The researcher may need to secure final agreements and final estimates of costs from others associated with the evaluation (for example, other organizations that are supplying information).

- Usually, the advisory committee (if you have one) meets to give their final okay to the work. This meeting might occur in person or via conference call.

Design
Step 5

Finalize and test methods

This step brings you into the nitty-gritty work of the design phase. When you conclude this step, you will be ready to begin your evaluation. In taking this step, you and the researcher test your measurement process (which you began to develop in step 3), refine the process as needed, and develop forms that program staff will use to gather information.

As a consumer of evaluation information, you should be satisfied at this point that measures selected for the evaluation have the five characteristics shown in Figure 10—relevance, validity, reliability, sensitivity, and timeliness.

Figure 10. Characteristics of Good Measures

Characteristic	Definition
Relevance	The measure is related to something important for your organization to know about.
Validity	The measure really measures what it is supposed to measure.
Reliability	The measure provides consistent, accurate "readings."
Sensitivity	The measure detects changes that you consider important.
Timeliness	The measure (and your plan for using it) provides information in time to be useful.

Relevance

You assess relevance by looking critically at a measure proposed for your evaluation research to determine whether it appears to provide the information you need. Relevance is very much a commonsense judgment on your part: will a measure result in information related to your needs? If you operate an in-home service program for the elderly, for example, asking about older people's satisfaction with life might be interesting information. However, it would not be relevant to your situation—unless your program has the goal to influence life satisfaction.

Validity

Validity (like reliability) comes from statistical literature. A measure is valid if it truly measures what it appears to measure. So, for example, suppose your program hopes to change the attitudes of young people regarding other cultures, and let's say that you are elated to discover an existing measurement scale labeled "Attitudes toward Cultures Scale." That measurement instrument would seem to be very relevant to your needs. Let's say that you happen to have a friend at a local academic institution who specializes in studies of cultural relations, and she knows everything there is to know about scales on this topic. If you ask her about it, and she states that research has demonstrated that this scale truly measures such attitudes, then you are in luck. It's valid. On the other hand, you might have the misfortune to learn, for example, that research has shown that the scores on this scale really just reflect how much people know about other cultures, not what they feel. In this case, it would not be a valid measure of cultural attitudes.

Reliability

A reliable measure is one that provides a consistent rating and is not susceptible to a great deal of error. For example, a reliable measurement tool will not provide a different result simply because measurements are taken at different times of day, or different days of the week, or by different staff who record the measurements.[22] A good example of a typically unreliable measure is asking staff who work in a program serving children and families to estimate, without reviewing internal records, how many of the program participants achieved certain goals in the past year. Such estimates suffer from the tendency of staff to give more weight to their recent, well-remembered experiences, rather than recalling what happened to the majority of families throughout the period of a year.

Sensitivity

Sensitivity refers to the ability of a measure to provide fine enough details. A sensitive measure is able to show changes that the program is attempting to make in participants in sufficient detail, if they occur. For example, a measure of student learning in a course must be aligned well enough with the subject matter being taught, and detailed enough, to detect before-after changes in students' understanding of the various topics covered. This can help the teacher to know which topics students are understanding well and which topics need more attention or a different approach to instruction.

Timeliness

Timeliness is simply a practical issue. You may have certain deadlines by which you need information in order to make changes in your program. Therefore, an adequate measure needs to be able to produce results by that time.

---

[22] Of course, some measurement instruments, such as clocks and calendars, should give different readings at different times, but that is another matter!

Roles of the researcher:

- Identify and obtain existing research measurement instruments, if they exist.[23]

- Design new research measurement instruments as needed.

- Look carefully at all data collection methods from an equity perspective and a culturally responsive evaluation perspective. Revise methods, if necessary.[24]

- Develop guidelines and instructions for collecting information.

- Train all persons involved in the testing of measures.

- Revise and retest methods until satisfied with their productivity.

Your roles:

- Review and comment on proposed methods.

- Inform staff of their responsibilities.

- Provide information regarding a sample for testing measures.

- Provide necessary materials, space, and supplies in accordance with the evaluation plan.

How this step usually occurs:

- Research staff work as much as possible on their own during this step.

- Your staff will be involved to whatever extent the design calls for their involvement. For example, your staff might assist in the selection of a sample to test survey questions. They then might contact people in the sample and ask if they will participate in testing the survey and, if they

---

[23] These may include survey questions that others have developed; they may include forms that you already have in place to collect information about the people you serve and what you do with them. In looking for measurement instruments that others might have developed, search for articles that have reviewed, summarized, and perhaps rated measurement tools for your topic. For example, the following article reviews family functioning measures: Rachel Pritchett, et al., "Quick, simple measures of family relationships for use in clinical practice and research. A systematic review." *Family Practice* 2011:28(2): 172–187.

[24] An informative set of principles and tools for focusing on racial equity in collecting and integrating community data and agency data appears in AISP, *Centering Racial Equity Throughout Data Integration* (Philadelphia,: University of Pennsylvania, 2020).

agree, provide their names to those conducting the survey. They also might organize records or collect information from existing records.[25]

Design Step 6 ➔

Train staff and implement the evaluation

This step is the transition from practice to the real thing. It comprises the time when all systems are go, and the countdown begins.

Roles of the researcher:

• Train data collectors, as appropriate.

• Closely monitor implementation and make adjustments as needed.

Your roles:

• Communicate, as necessary, about the evaluation with all appropriate parties. These may include staff in your organization, the people your organization serves, staff from other organizations that will be asked to participate in the evaluation in any way, and any others who need to know about the evaluation.

• Train your staff related to their responsibilities within the evaluation. (If the evaluation researcher will do this, then just facilitate the process as necessary.)

How this step usually occurs:

• As with Design Step 5, research staff work as much as possible on their own during this step.

• Your staff will be involved in the evaluation to whatever extent required by the evaluation design. For example, your staff might assist in the selection of a sample, contact people about participating in a survey, provide names of people who agree to participate in a survey, and organize records or collect information from existing records.

With Design Step 6 underway, the evaluation moves on to the data collection phase.

---

[25] To learn more about the activities associated with steps 3, 4, 5, and 6, see "Practical Data Collection" in Leonard Bickman and Debra J. Rog, eds., *Handbook of Applied Social Research Methods* (Thousand Oaks, CA: Sage, 2009). It is thorough, provides more details than we can discuss here, yet is quite readable with a minimum of jargon.

CASE EXAMPLE:

Using Existing Tools and Creating Your Own

What's the study?

Hmong Karen Youth Pride program evaluation

Topic of study:

Youth development, cultural identity, language learning

What were the evaluation study questions?

Do student participants…

- Maintain or increase their Hmong or Karen literacy skills?
- Maintain or increase their knowledge about their own culture?
- Talk to their parents or family members about their Hmong or Karen culture or history?
- Build positive relationships with adults and peers in the program?

Methods used:

Youth surveys, parent focus groups, reading assessments

How was it done?

Wilder Research developed a survey for students and a focus group protocol for parents of students. In addition, staff at Hmong Karen Youth Pride assessed students at the beginning and end of their six-week program using the Hmong Reading Assessment and the Karen Sight Words Assessment. The Hmong Reading Assessment is used by the local school district to assess Hmong reading proficiency in Hmong-English dual language programs; this assessment tool was developed by the school district. Similarly, the Karen Sight Words Assessment was an existing assessment tool that the researchers utilized for the evaluation; this assessment tool was developed by the Hmong Karen Youth Pride program.

What's the takeaway?

Evaluations can benefit from existing tools. Existing tools are sometimes tested and validated by research experts, so you know that they will collect good data. If these tools are used widely enough, there may be a database of findings from similar evaluations that you can use for comparison purposes. If you plan to use an existing tool, make sure you get permission to use it and that you know its strengths and limitations.

Other times, you will need to create your own tools for your evaluation. This is beneficial because you can tailor the tool for exactly what you want to learn. In this example, the researchers created their own tools as well as used existing tools. However, take care in developing new tools to be certain that they have reliability, validity, and the other characteristics of good measures discussed earlier. If they lack those features, you will not have good data for decision-making.

ANOTHER CASE EXAMPLE:

Using Existing Tools and Creating Your Own

What's the study?

Invest Early evaluation

Topic of study:

Early childhood, rural areas

What were the evaluation study questions?

The study wanted to learn...

- What makes Invest Early successful, and what improvements are needed?
- How does Invest Early compare to the state of early childhood programming nationally?

Methods used:

Child development and school readiness assessments, classroom and home observations, parent surveys and interviews, community discussions

How was it done?

Wilder Research developed a number of tools, including a parent survey, a parent interview protocol, a parenting observation protocol, and a community discussion protocol. The researchers also identified and used existing tools, such as the Social Support for School Readiness survey (developed by Invest Early), the Home Observation for Measuring Environment (developed by Bettye Caldwell and Robert Bradley), and the Classroom Assessment Scoring System (developed by the School Center for Advanced Study of Teaching and Learning).

What's the takeaway?

The existing tools have been used widely throughout the US, and they have been tested and validated extensively. This meant that the researchers could trust the data these tools collected and that there were many examples of how to use these tools in evaluations. Also, by using these tools, this study contributed to the body of knowledge about early childhood and school readiness.

The researchers also opted to create some tools of their own because the existing tools wouldn't provide them with all of the information they needed. The choice between developing your own tools or using existing tools often depends on the evaluation questions and your program's context.

Data Collection Phase

Even in this age of sophisticated technology, the collection of data remains a very human, very manual process. Some person, at some point in the process, must write something down or strike a keyboard. The potential for human error looms large. In the data collection phase of your work, you must attempt to ensure that whatever gets recorded represents "reality" as closely as possible.

Somebody might complete a questionnaire; two people (an interviewer and a respondent) might ask and answer questions; someone might tape record and transcribe a meeting; someone might respond to questions online; someone might observe an activity and record their observations on a rating form. In each case, people think. People make judgments. People strive to tell the truth, and people sometimes try to paint an image of reality that differs from what really exists. People make mistakes.

We cannot improve the quality of data once those data have been collected. High-powered computers and complex statistical analysis cannot transform incorrect information into correct information. They cannot create data that nobody collected in the first place.[26]

What is the major lesson? During the data collection phase, you must emphasize the importance of gathering the data you need in a reliable, credible manner. If you don't, your study may have very limited, or even no, value.

The data collection phase has three steps:

• Data Collection Step 1: Obtain necessary information using methods developed during the design phase.

• Data Collection Step 2: Clean data.

• Data Collection Step 3: Compile and store data.

---

[26] This does not imply that we cannot do "estimates" to try to portray what's missing or to correct what's wrong. In fact, you might have heard about statistical programs which "impute" data to fill in for an item or two that a data set lacks for a specific respondent. But that is another process, and one which obviously is not as desirable as having the right information there from the start. It also introduces additional statistical complications.

Data Collection
Step 1 ➡

Obtain necessary information using methods developed during the design phase[27]

This is when people complete forms, take part in surveys, or do other data collection activities necessary to obtain information.

Roles of the researcher:

- Collect information. In some cases, researchers will do this on their own; in other cases, they have assistants who gather the necessary information through interviews, mailed surveys, focus groups, observations, or whatever appropriate means.

Your roles:

- Make your records available, as needed, to provide data already collected and to provide contact information for people who will participate in the evaluation study.

- Your staff may gather and record information, by completing forms or doing assessments, for example.

How this step usually occurs:

- Research staff conduct surveys, carry out focus groups, review and tabulate information from records, as needed.

Your staff is involved to the extent specified in the design.

Data Collection
Step 2 ➡

Clean data

This step involves checking and correcting information—making sure that information is as complete and accurate as possible.

Roles of the researcher:

- Research staff inspect data to make sure they are accurate.

- Research staff make corrections, as appropriate.

---

[27] A readable, mildly technical description of major concepts and activities related to data collection, analysis and reporting appears in Marvin C. Alkin, *Evaluation Essentials: A to Z* (New York: Guilford Press, 2011). The book offers a nice overview, oriented toward the teaching of evaluation research, with descriptions of greater depth than in this *Manager's Guide to Program Evaluation*.

- Sometimes, people who provided information or who responded to surveys receive a call to clarify an ambiguity or to provide data that had been omitted.

Your role:

- Usually no effort on your part, other than occasionally to respond to questions the research staff might have for you.

How this step usually occurs:

- Deep in the heart of "Data Central," your researchers work with the study data.

Compile and store data

Data Collection
Step 3

In some way or another, the information you have gathered for your evaluation study has to be compiled and stored. Sometimes data are stored in an Excel file; other times they are stored in your organization's data tracking software; other times still, they are stored in actual physical files—pieces of paper organized so that you can readily find pertinent evaluation information when necessary. Whether you put the information into a computer or organize it on pages of paper, you need something that is coherent and that you can efficiently consult and analyze to draw conclusions.

Roles of the researcher:

- Code data. If data collection involved open-ended questions that allowed study participants to respond however they wished, that information needs to be put into a coherent, analyzable form. Most typically, this involves the development of a coding system to categorize responses for later statistical tallying and analysis. Sometimes categories exist ahead of time for coding (from previous evaluation research, for instance). Other times the categories emerge from the review of the data. Software programs can also assist with coding.[28]

- Enter data into a data file for analysis, as appropriate. In most cases, this compilation of data involves constructing a computerized data file. In

---

[28] A very comprehensive overview of approaches to coding responses to open-ended questions and other qualitative information appears in Johnny Saldaña, *The Coding Manual for Qualitative Researchers*, 3rd edition (Thousand Oaks, CA: Sage, 2016). Many different software options exist for coding. Do a web search for "qualitative data analysis options."

limited cases for small-scale studies, data may simply remain on paper for tabulation by hand.

Your role:

- You might advise or collaborate in the construction of codes for organizing text and qualitative information.

- Otherwise, usually very little effort on your part.

How this step usually occurs:

- Those eccentric researchers take care of it.

- Once data are compiled and stored, this phase has ended. It's time to analyze the data.

Analysis Phase

In this phase, you look at the information you have collected and determine its implications. There are two steps within the analysis phase:

Analysis Step 1: Conduct initial analysis.

Analysis Step 2: Review and finalize the analysis.

Analysis
Step 1 ➲

Conduct initial analysis

Here, the evaluators tally findings, look at differences among groups, and try to determine how different bits of information relate to one another.

Roles of the researcher:

- Develop descriptive statistics that summarize all the information gathered through the study. Perform analysis as required to answer the study questions. This could include an examination of differences between different types of clients, or comparing findings about your program to other programs or benchmarks. As an example of the first case, the initial analysis may have shown you that, overall, 88 percent of the people you serve are satisfied. However, you might want to know if satisfaction is greater among women than men, or greater among Jamaicans than

Puerto Ricans. As an example of the second case (comparative findings), the researcher might bring Census data into the analysis in some way. If your program addressed needs at a community level, the researcher might find other communities to compare with yours. Analysis might also include comparing participants' functioning or needs at program entry with their functioning or needs shortly after they complete the program. For example, participants' employment status might be compared before and after receiving program services intended to improve their employment prospects.[29]

Your role:
- Again, very little. You probably feel a bit lazy by now, and maybe you even forget what the researcher looks like—but remain vigilant. You play an important part in the next step.

How this step usually occurs:
- The researcher analyzes information using appropriate statistical methods.

Review and finalize the analysis

In this step, you will look at findings, discuss and critique them, and typically ask for more analysis, until you feel you have answered your evaluation questions. During this step, it is important to have an open mind, be inquisitive, and consider findings from all points of view. You can invite others to participate in the review as well. In this way, you will produce the most instructive and most credible research findings.

Analysis
Step 2

Roles of the researcher:
- Bring drafts of findings to you and others for review.

- Provide preliminary interpretations and suggestions for action.

- Facilitate in-depth discussion of findings, interpretations, and suggestions for action.

---

[29] In performing any of these comparative analyses, the researcher will typically carry out tests of statistical significance. Chapter 5 mentions a bit more about such tests.

- Listen to your comments and return to Analysis Step 1 for additional statistical processing, as needed, to respond to your questions and suggestions.

Your roles:

- Carefully review findings.

- React to findings and give ideas for the final report.

- Call together your advisors, some staff from your program, and consultants if you have them to help with the review.

How this step usually occurs:

- One or more meetings between you and the researcher.

- One or more meetings of the advisory committee, if you have one, or of other stakeholders you call together.[30]

---

[30] During this phase, you share preliminary findings and possibly share report drafts with a limited number of people. Findings are clearly labeled as "for discussion only, not for distribution," since they may change as a result of further analysis. This sharing of findings differs from the Reporting Phase where you share final results with as many audiences as you consider appropriate.

CASE EXAMPLE:

The Benefits of Qualitative Methods

What's the study?

American Indian Youth Enrichment program evaluation

Topic of study:

Youth development, cultural identity

What were the evaluation study questions?

- Did students feel safe and supported in the program?
- Did students improve at completing schoolwork regularly?
- Did students have positive feelings regarding their American Indian culture?
- How satisfied were parents and grandparents with the program?

Methods used:

Student interviews, program observations, and talking circles with parents and grandparents

How was it done?

Wilder Research conducted the interviews, observations, and talking circles, and then mapped the findings onto two frameworks for thinking about basic needs: Maslow's Hierarchy of Needs and Cross's Inter-Relational Worldview. The main difference between these frameworks is that Maslow's focuses on individual needs and Cross's focuses on collective needs. For the American Indian Youth Empowerment program, Cross's framework better communicated how they view their work—that is, as part of a wider community of support rather than as operating in isolation. The researchers began the evaluation expecting to use Maslow's framework throughout; however, because they used qualitative methods, they were able to see that Cross's framework better aligned with how students and their family members talked about their experiences with the program.

What's the takeaway?

Especially for first-time studies or exploratory studies, evaluations can benefit from the use of qualitative methods. Qualitative methods allow for participants to speak in their own words and talk about whatever is most meaningful to them about a program. This means that the researcher gains invaluable knowledge about how participants view a program and the impact it has on their life.

In contrast, quantitative methods often use predetermined response options (such as multiple choice questions in surveys), so participants cannot always respond in their own words—so it is very important that the researcher knows a lot about a program before creating such a survey to evaluate it. If not, the researcher risks missing important information about the impacts of the program for participants.

Reporting Phase

In this phase, you share findings with the intended users of the information as well as with other stakeholders whom you consider appropriate. There are two steps:

- Reporting Step 1: Present findings to intended audiences in both oral and written forms.

- Reporting Step 2: Make other presentations as needed.

Reporting Step 1

Present findings to intended audiences in both oral and written forms

With this step, you and others receive the official findings. There should not be any surprises because you already reviewed the preliminary findings. However, that does not mean you will like the findings. The researcher has done a job as an independent professional, which means they produce findings according to best practices for evaluation research—not according to whether you or others will like the findings.

Roles of the researcher:
- Produce a report that includes, at a minimum, a brief description of the program being evaluated and a list of the evaluation questions; a description of the findings of the evaluation research; an interpretation of the findings; suggestions for future action; and a description of the methods used, including the strengths and limitations of the methods.

- Present and discuss findings with you and other intended audiences.

Your roles:
- Receive the report.

- Participate in discussions.

- Initiate steps to put the evaluation findings to use—to improve your program, influence policy, obtain funding, or other uses that are important to you. This is data-informed decision making.

How this step usually occurs:

- Advisory committee meets, if you have one, to discuss the evaluation results.

- Presentations to staff and others intended to receive the results.

- Production of a written report. The content, format, and length of the written report will differ depending on whether the evaluation involves a one-time look at a program or a point-in-time snapshot based on ongoing evaluation of your program.

  - For a one-time evaluation: The report will include pages of text, tables, and graphs, including all of the components listed above (under "role of the researcher").

  - For an ongoing evaluation: The report might appear in the form of just data tables, produced on a regular basis (e.g., semi-annually), with notes describing the information. Other information about the evaluation, including a description of the methods, recommendations, etc. might exist in separate documents or on slides prepared for meetings.

Make other presentations as needed

Reporting
↻ Step 2

The work done to evaluate your program may have relevance to others. You may feel that your program's research should have an influence on policy and practice within your field. If so, then you may want to share the findings locally and nationally, with colleagues in similar organizations, with funders, public officials, professional networks, academic institutions, and others.[31]

---

[31] Books have been written about the dissemination of research findings, how to go about it, and what influences the use of findings by program developers and policy makers. See, for example: chapters by Iwaniec, Pinkerton, and Kelly in *Making Research Work*, edited by Dorothy Iwaniec and John Pinkerton (Chichester, England: John Wiley & Sons, 1998); Paul W. Mattessich, Donald W. Compton, and Michael Baizerman, "Evaluation Use and the Collaborative Evaluation Fellows Project," *Cancer Practice* 2001:9: 85–91; Valerie J. Caracelli and Hallie Preskill, *The Expanding Scope of Evaluation Use* (San Francisco: Jossey-Bass, 2000); Advice appears in Centers for Disease Control and Prevention. *Evaluation Reporting: A Guide to Help Ensure Use of Evaluation Findings*, Atlanta: US Department of Health and Human Services; 2013. Adrienne E. Adams, et al., "'Expectations to Change' (E2C): A Participatory Method for Facilitating Stakeholder Engagement with Evaluation Findings." *American Journal of Evaluation* 2015:36(2): 243–255 describe a six-step process for bringing evaluation research findings to stakeholders in order to support the formulation of action steps to bring about programmatic change.

If you want your evaluation to have an impact beyond improving the effectiveness of your organization's services, you want to make sure that, starting at the very beginning of the design phase, you have made your evaluation relevant to others and you have carried it out in the most credible way. If you want to increase the likelihood that others will use the results of your work to improve their programs and to promote positive change in communities, you should:

- Provide actionable results—results that are practical and that others can implement.

- Present results clearly to people who can use them and who want to advocate for change in communities or systems.

- Report your work so that it informs organizations who seek to reduce disparities, meet the needs of disadvantaged or underserved people, or empower marginalized members of society.

- Use professional journals and the media to communicate your findings.[32]

Roles of the researcher:
- Produce additional reports of study findings.

- Present findings at meetings and conferences.[33]

Your roles:
- Identify audiences who would benefit from your findings or with whom you want to share your findings.

- Set up meetings or presentations with those audiences.

---

[32] James R. Cook, "Using Evaluation to Effect Social Change: Looking Through a Community Psychology Lens." *American Journal of Evaluation* 2014:36(1): 107–117, presents ten strategies, including the strategies listed here, for doing evaluation in a way that promotes positive community change.

[33] The presentations and reports in this step of the work have a cost. If resources have not been built into the final agreement (during Design Step 4), they need to be committed before the work commences on these extra reports and presentations. Such presentations can have important, mission-related benefits for your organization (for example, to influence public policy, change standard practices, create positive public relations, or attract new funding).

- Commit necessary funding for presentations and reports.

- Participate in presentations. (Do them yourself, if you like!)

- Collaborate on additional reports from the evaluation, if interested and appropriate.

How this step usually occurs:

- A public report, and sometimes a press release, is written and distributed.

- Meetings are held with media representatives.

- Presentations are made at a special meeting or conference related to the findings.

Time-Limited Projects vs. Ongoing Evaluation

The description of four research phases may appear to apply only to time-limited studies, such as a one-time program evaluation that may last about two years, report its findings, and not continue beyond that time.

However, the phases also apply to ongoing evaluation research—that is, evaluation that gathers and reports information indefinitely, as a constant resource for program improvement. In this case, the design phase repeats itself periodically as a review activity. The later phases continue uninterrupted, on schedule, subject to change only if the latest design work makes alterations of any type.

Ongoing evaluation offers routine opportunities for interpreting information on activities, outputs, and outcomes. That interpretation can lead to changes in a program.

Summary

The steps described in this chapter comprise the sequence of events that occur in all program evaluations in some way, shape, or form. The chapter has offered you an understanding of program evaluation activities and has alerted you to what you can typically expect at different phases of a program evaluation. The chapter identified certain roles as "yours" and certain roles as belonging to "the researcher."

Of course, you still need to decide what evaluation steps you will do on your own and what you will hire someone else to do. Therefore, in the next chapter, we discuss the staffing of evaluation research, describe various options you might consider for consultants, and offer suggestions for making your relationship with an evaluation consultant as productive and satisfying as possible. We also look at other practical issues such as costs and contracting.

4

Staffing the Evaluation and Estimating Costs

"Should we hire someone, or do this on our own? Or both?"

No universal answer exists for this question. In honesty, it depends upon many factors. For example:

• What capability do you and your staff have to do the work?

• How complicated is the process of measuring what you need to measure?

• Are you starting from scratch, or does a system already exist that can provide much of the information you need?

As you would if you wanted to construct or repair a home, you have to make a decision based on your abilities and your priorities. Most people could not design and build their own home, but some can do so. Many people can do minor repairs in their homes, but they call a plumber, electrician, or other professional for major work. Some people can do construction or repair work effectively, but they lack the time necessary to complete the job. Circumstances matter.

Figure 11 lists some options and the circumstances that might lead you to select each option as the best for you.

Figure 11. Options for Staffing the Evaluation

Option	Considerations
Do the work completely on your own: design the evaluation, collect your data, analyze the data, and report your findings. (No use of a consultant at all.)	• Your staff includes a person (perhaps yourself) who has sufficient evaluation knowledge for necessary design and oversight of the work. Some organizations have an "internal program evaluator" or someone on staff whose job it is to manage data-related tasks, such as evaluation.* • You have the time and other resources to do the work. • Staff in your organization can assist as needed with data collection, data analysis, and reporting of findings. • All or most of the information that you need comes from an existing electronic record system that you manage or otherwise have access to.
Hire a consultant only for design or other selected portions of the work. Do the other portions of the work on your own. Then, hire a consultant occasionally for dealing with problems and advice on expanding or making changes to your evaluation work.	• You and your staff have the necessary skills for some evaluation activities but not for others. For example, you are not familiar with the necessary methods or data sources. • You and your staff don't have the time to design a new evaluation process or system. • You have staff who can implement and maintain a system, with a little advice and coaching from an expert, after the system has been designed.
Hire a consultant to handle all phases of the work.	• You lack the staff, the capability, the time, or other resources to do the work.

* An internal program evaluator has training in the methods necessary to accomplish a good evaluation. For ideas related to making internal evaluation effective, see Paul W Mattessich, et al., "Managing Evaluation for Program Improvement." *New Directions for Evaluation* 2016:121: 27–42.

Some other considerations may motivate you to use a consultant. In a sense, these are "overriding factors." Whether or not you have the necessary experience, staff, time, or other resources to do the evaluation on your own, these circumstances take precedence:

- *The need for objectivity and neutrality.* You may need to make sure that some or all of the primary audiences for your evaluation have confidence that the work was done by someone with no affiliation or vested interest in your organization and its programs.

- *Requirements of your funders.* Organizations that provide you with funds may require that you participate in an evaluation conducted by a third party. They may do this for purposes of objectivity, but they may also do it as part of a larger effort to accumulate and combine common evaluation findings from multiple programs that they fund.

Please note that cost and available funds do not appear in these considerations. It would be irresponsible to suggest that you should do the work on your own solely because you need to save money or that you should hire a consultant just because you have some extra funds in your bank account. You first must decide which options can produce high-quality and meaningful evaluation findings for you and your stakeholders. After you have identified the options that can produce a quality product, you can then use cost, as well as other features, to help you make your final decision. If hiring a consultant is the only way that you can meet your evaluation goals, but you don't have any money to do so, then you will need either to obtain the necessary funds through a grant or find some other way of financing the work.

CASE EXAMPLE:

Dividing Evaluation Tasks between Researchers and Program Staff

What's the study?

Women's Recovery Services program evaluation

Topic of study:

Addiction treatment and recovery, mental and physical health, basic needs and daily living

What were the evaluation study questions?

To what extent does participation in the program result in...

- Women reducing their use of drugs and alcohol, or maintaining sobriety?
- Women increasing their ability to achieve other outcomes, such as housing, employment, parenting, or physical and mental health outcomes?

Methods used:

Client intake and exit forms, client program contact form, client urinary analysis testing, client pregnancy outcome form, client interviews

How was it done?

Wilder Research developed an evaluation plan that provided guidance to program staff as they collected most of the data themselves. Wilder Research developed client intake and exit forms, a client program contact form, client urinary analysis testing, and a client pregnancy outcome form, along with instructions. The client intake and exit forms collected demographic information and information about services and referrals. The client program contact form collected the amount of direct contact that clients had with the program. The urinary analysis testing served to determine if clients were using substances. The pregnancy outcome form collected mother and baby health data at birth.

The researchers also developed a client interview protocol, which they used to conduct interviews with clients at one month, six months, and twelve months after they exited the program. These interviews captured longitudinal information about clients' substance use, access to social support, physical and mental health, their children's health and well-being, parenting and their relationship with their children, housing and employment status, and their satisfaction with the program.

What's the takeaway?

Dividing evaluation tasks between researchers and program staff can improve evaluation efficiency as well as decrease the financial burden of hiring a consultant for your evaluation. In this case example, the researchers leveraged the program's existing documentation procedures (such as client intake and exit) as opportunities to gather evaluation data. Since program staff led these procedures, they fulfilled a crucial role in the evaluation—for example, gathering demographic data, services data, and referral data. As you plan your evaluation, think strategically about which tasks your program staff could do and which tasks would be better accomplished by your researcher.

Selecting a Research Consultant

Some insightful stories regarding the use of consultants come from people I've met over the years:

• Someone whose organization expected a group of university students to do an evaluation study as a class project "for free," only to learn to their dismay that the school semester did not allow enough time to complete the work required. So, they ended up with only a literature review.

• Someone from an organization who hired an evaluator who promised a "thorough qualitative evaluation that will explore the program in depth." What they received was a set of good, narrative stories. This greatly disappointed their funders who appreciated the stories, but who also expected basic facts that indicated how many people participated in the program, how many completed it, which ones seemed to benefit from it, which ones didn't, and why.

• Someone whose organization was impressed by the comprehensiveness of a research proposal from a large, international accounting firm. They paid a great deal of money for the work. However, in the end, they felt the final product did not meet their needs. The reasons for this failure to meet their needs, they suspected, were that the consultants had no experience working with small nonprofit organizations, and the specific model the consultants applied to the project had originated within a business school framework for use with for-profit organizations.

What do these illustrations teach us? They do *not* imply that large accounting firms, university students, or qualitative evaluators cannot do the kind of research you want them to do. In fact, they can all do excellent research under the right circumstances.

Each of these unfortunate situations ended badly because a research consultant did not understand an organization's evaluation needs. The organizations themselves did not effectively state or communicate their evaluation needs during the consultant selection process. The consultants did not ask all necessary questions. The unspoken evaluation needs of these organizations included: (1) their timeline for the evaluation, (2) the information they needed to report to their funder, and (3) the relatively small size of their organization and the realities of working in the nonprofit sector.

So, the major lesson from these examples: look carefully at the consulting vendors available to you and determine how well each of them can meet the needs you currently have. Regardless of how well or poorly various consultants have worked with you or others before, the question you should raise is: does a consultant have the ability to work with us now and meet the needs we currently have? You need to match your specific needs with the capability of the consultant.

In the next few sections, we will discuss some general principles that you might keep in mind when selecting a consultant.

Types of evaluation research vendors

It's hard to categorize and make generalizations about types of evaluation research vendors—any attempt misrepresents some of the people placed in a category. Nevertheless, over the years, I have noticed certain traits that tend to distinguish one type of consultant from another. You need to understand these in order to make the best decision about the person and organization with whom you would like to work.

Independent professionals, working alone. This includes freelance consultants, solo practitioners—people who operate on their own. They may have a small staff of clerical and research assistants. However, only a very small proportion of them have employees who specialize in things such as statistical analysis, database management, and survey interviewing. In small projects, they tend to do all the work themselves; in larger, more complex projects, they subcontract with others for portions of the work. They may or may not limit themselves to working with nonprofit organizations.

Research/consulting organizations, not for profit. This includes freestanding research organizations as well as research groups that are part of a larger organization, such as a service provider or a foundation. These organizations may have anywhere from a few research staff to several hundred. Almost always they have research support staff (research assistants, statistical analysts, database managers). Usually, they have the capacity to do surveys on their own (web, phone, and mailed) up to a certain scale. Beyond that, they often subcontract or decline projects. These organizations often dedicate themselves only to program evaluation. Sometimes, they also limit the focus of their work to a specific topic. Sometimes, they do both evaluation and other forms of applied research (research intended to assist in the development of programs, policies, or other activities). Typically, they specialize in work with nonprofit organizations; if they work with for-profit organizations at all, they usually do so only for projects with a "public benefit." For example, such an organization might decline to do work for a bank if the proposed project focused on customer marketing issues. However, if the same bank approached it to do a study of a program intended to help low-income residents increase their resources in order to buy a home, then the organization might accept the project.

Research/consulting organizations, for profit. This includes organizations similar in characteristics to the nonprofit research/consulting organizations. However, they usually do not specialize in work for nonprofit organizations and public benefit projects. In fact, they often emphasize work with for-profit clients and government agencies. For the larger firms, evaluation and other forms of applied research often constitute only a small proportion of their work. Some of these for-profit research/consulting organizations offer a limited amount of pro bono work to nonprofit organizations.

Academic research centers/university faculty. This includes academic centers that formally offer services, as well as faculty who work essentially independently but under the auspices of a university.[34] Such centers may include just a few faculty or virtually everyone in the university, depending upon how they market their services. They also often have some graduate students who serve as research consultants. They typically have staff and students with varying levels of experience and skills related to statistics, data processing, interviewing, and other research activities. They often have established relationships with a survey research center in their institution for survey work.

Figure 12 lists each of the four types of vendors, along with a very general assessment of their positives and negatives. The figure can serve as a starting guide to help you know what to look for, what to be cautious about, and what to probe for as you talk to various research vendors. However,

---

[34] A university faculty member who does his or her work outside of the auspices of the university, essentially as a separate job, would fit more appropriately into the first category, "independent professionals, working alone."

when you make your actual decision, you should consider each consulting option you have on its own merits. Obviously, in your decision-making, you will want to assess the general features of vendors listed below with specific information you have obtained about each of your candidates. For example, you should consider their experience, their reputation (if you can speak with some others about them), their proposed evaluation approach, the way they presented themselves when you interviewed them, and the likelihood that they can tailor their services to your specific needs.

Figure 12. Pros and Cons of Vendor Types

Type of Vendor	Positives	Negatives
Independent professionals, working alone	• Can often offer more customized attention and more time than other vendors • May specialize in just your field	• May lack close access to specialists and peers for obtaining advice and sharing work • Not full service; can't do all phases on their own (other than for simple or small projects) • Sometimes can't do large projects
Research/consulting organizations, not for profit	• Nonprofit mission (understand nonprofit organization culture) • Often full-service capacity—can do all phases of work • Large number of staff, often including specialists and content experts	• Sometimes can't do small projects • Sometimes stretched for resources to meet the demands placed on them
Research/consulting organizations, for profit	• Often full-service capacity—can do all phases of work • Large number of staff, often including specialists and content experts	• Often not interested in working with nonprofit organizations • May be expensive • Sometimes can't do small projects
Academic research centers, university faculty	• Credibility of their institution strengthens the image of your work • Often full service	• May be more interested in their agenda than yours (very common complaint) • Not always full service

What Should You Look For in a Consultant?

Following are questions to ask (and characteristics to look for) as you interview evaluation consultants.

- Will the consultant tailor the process to fit your needs? Do they bring a cookie-cutter or "one size fits all" approach? Does the consultant ask questions that indicate flexibility in design and approach?

- Will the consultant provide you with <u>both</u> complete, relevant, and reliable data <u>and</u> stories that illustrate what the data show —so that you and your stakeholders have a sound basis for making decisions?

- Does the consultant seek information about important features of the context in which the evaluation project will occur? Do they take culture and race into account? Do they understand the pace of work in the program? Do they understand community conditions that might affect how information can be collected?

- Does the consultant think strategically to understand the connections among the evaluation, your short-term and long-term goals, and other issues your organization faces?

- Does the consultant share your perspective on considerations of equity, power, and community engagement in evaluation?

- Does the consultant seek to understand the variety of audiences the evaluation will serve? In what ways do they indicate an understanding of how the results can be used with various audiences and for various purposes?

- Does the consultant have experience commensurate with the project tasks, including familiarity with populations similar to those you serve and knowledge about issues the evaluation will likely face? Has the consultant worked with organizations similar to yours?

- Is the consultant currently available with the capacity to do the work when you need it done?

- Does the consultant's work style fit with your needs?

- Do you have a good rapport with and good feelings about the consultant?

- Are you confident about the impression this consultant (or their assistants) will make when speaking with your clients, board, staff, funders, volunteers, or other important constituents?

Let the buyer beware

Evaluators come from many different backgrounds—a fact that the journal *Evaluation and Program Planning* states as a guiding principle:

> *Evaluation and Program Planning is based on the principle that the techniques and methods of evaluation and planning transcend the boundaries of specific fields and that relevant contributions to these areas come from people representing many different positions, intellectual traditions, and interests.*

In my opinion, the wise consumer, after reading this principle, should say: "Let the buyer beware." This advice does not imply that incompetent and unscrupulous evaluation professionals prey upon unsuspecting people such as yourself. However, it does recognize that the title of "evaluator" does not suggest a common base of skills, knowledge, or approaches to research design.

The field of accounting, in contrast, has established that all accountants subscribe to at least a minimal common set of concepts. New accountants are trained in those concepts; if someone has an accounting degree, the consumer knows that they received such training. A national Financial Accounting Standards Board rules on accounting standards, rules, practices, and methods with the force of law. No similar testing or credentialing mechanism has emerged within the evaluation profession in the United States.[35] The Canadian Evaluation Society does have a process for awarding the status of "Credentialed Evaluator," stating, "The holder of the CE designation has provided convincing evidence of the requisite skills, knowledge and practical experience identified by the CES as those necessary to be a competent evaluator."[36]

---

[35] See James W. Altschuld, "The Certification of Evaluators: Highlights from a Report Submitted to the Board of Directors of the American Evaluation Association," *American Journal of Evaluation* 1999:20:: 481–93; and Steven C. Jones and Blaine R. Worthen, "AEA Members' Opinions Concerning Evaluator Certification," *American Journal of Evaluation* 1999:20: 495–506. These articles outline the pros and cons of a certification process and revealed, as of the end of the twentieth century, little consensus among professional evaluators concerning the need for such certification—a lack of consensus that has persisted to the present day. Randall Davies, et al., ("Using Open Badges to Certify Practicing Evaluators." *American Journal of Evaluation* 2017:36(2): 151–163) suggested the use of open badges, but their suggestion has not gained traction in the US. The European Evaluation Society has developed a peer review and badge program for evaluators. In 2018, the American Evaluation Association approved "Evaluator Competencies." See: Jean A. King, "The American Evaluation Association's Program Evaluator Competencies" (*New Directions for Evaluation*, 168, 2020), for competencies recommended by the American Evaluation Association.

[36] See "About the CE Designation", https://evaluationcanada.ca/ce

Finding an Evaluation Consultant

Three common methods for finding an evaluation consultant are word of mouth, contacting the state chapter of the American Evaluation Association, and advertising through a request for proposals (RFP). Each of these has its positive and negative features. They are not mutually exclusive; you might combine any or all of them. A brief discussion of these methods appears below.

Word of mouth

You can always ask people you know in other organizations to identify evaluation consultants with whom they have worked. If your network is limited, contact people in your field and allied fields, introduce yourself, and ask whether they have used an evaluation consultant who they can recommend. Ask how well the consultant performed and obtain at least a general understanding of the consultant's approach to see if it will be compatible with your approach.

Personal referrals have great value. Their drawback is that they limit you to what the members of your professional network know about evaluation researchers.

Contacting the state chapter of the American Evaluation Association

Most states have a chapter of the American Evaluation Association. Chapters are typically organized and managed by one or more evaluators who volunteer for this task. Chapters have lists of members, and most chapters will provide access to this list for people who want to hire an evaluation consultant.

The use of an American Evaluation Association chapter has the major advantage of linking you to a network of consultants wider than you probably could have identified on your own. However, as previously noted, membership in the American Evaluation Association does not indicate that a person has achieved any sort of certification. In addition, it does not imply any common set of standards or approaches to evaluation. You should always screen carefully for a potential evaluation consultant's experience, skills, and alignment with your needs.

Advertising through a request for proposals

Organizations seeking an evaluation consultant frequently issue requests for proposals (RFPs). They may send these to a few or a large number of consultants. Sometimes they obtain a mailing list from their state American Evaluation Association chapter for this purpose. Sometimes, they solicit names and addresses by word of mouth. Occasionally, the use of an RFP (and associated evaluation) is mandated by a funding body as a condition of receiving grant money for a program.

Developing and sending an RFP to prospective vendors of evaluation services has advantages for you and for the consultant. For you, the process of developing the RFP and reviewing proposals you receive in response to it will help you to clarify your expectations for the evaluation. You will receive information from interested consultants in a standard format that will facilitate apples-to-apples comparisons among different vendors. A good RFP enables consultants to know what you expect and approximately when you expect it. The RFP often gives them enough information to determine whether their interests and qualifications match the job. Thus, they can decide whether to consider the work without wasting your time and theirs trying to construct a general picture of what the project will entail.

Creating an RFP

The typical components of an RFP include:

- A description of your organization: name, location, size, mission.

- A description of the program to be evaluated: goals, major activities, number and types of persons who participate in it.

- A statement of the outcomes expected from the program, to the extent that you know them now. (You may develop or refine these outcomes with the consultant.)

- A summary description of the work you would like the evaluator to do. This part of the RFP provides the consultant with a general picture of your expectations as you know them at the present time.

- Any practical considerations that will affect the consultant's decision whether to bid on the work and the consultant's decisions about the best approach to propose. These may include important deadlines, cost considerations, or special requirements your organization has related to doing program evaluation research.

- Consultant qualifications, if you have any characteristics that you feel are essential.

- Guidelines for the content of the proposal—what you want included, such as: the consultant's evaluation or research experience with similar programs; proposed evaluation design and methods, data collection, data analysis, and reporting of findings; proposed work plan; and costs.

- Submission requirements, including person and address or email to which the proposal must be submitted, date by which the proposal must be submitted, maximum length (if any), and required format (if any).

Productive Use of Evaluation Consultants

Of course, the principles of good relationships that apply to your daily interaction also apply to relationships with evaluators. In addition, here is some specific advice, based on many years of observing interpersonal dynamics between program managers and evaluation researchers.

- Have a program theory. You don't need a perfectly formed theory before you start working with an evaluator. In fact, you could build one as part of your work together. However, you should be committed to having such a theory, because it will instantly communicate much of what the evaluator needs to know about things that need to be measured. Also, it will enhance your thinking about your program and, consequently, your ability to communicate both with the evaluator and with others.

- Intend to *use* the results of the evaluation. Develop a conscious plan for this, if possible. You will greatly increase the productivity of the evaluation if you keep your eye on how you want to use the results. This will improve the quality of the research design.

- Make your expectations as clear as possible. Clarify what the project should accomplish. If you have unclear expectations, you will likely achieve only frustration.

- Focus on the information needs of the users of the project's results. Make sure that you have considered what all intended users want to get from the study.[37]

- Develop a good advisory committee (if appropriate). Advisory committees can inject insight and energy into projects. By having representatives from groups expected to use the information, you ensure that the design addresses their needs.

- Consider every step to be a collaborative work in progress. The better you carry out your roles in working together with the evaluator, the more likely that your needs will be met and the evaluation product will be useful.

- Budget enough time (for the design and for the work itself). Especially among people who have not had much experience with evaluation, it is quite common to grossly underestimate the amount of time it will take to design and implement good evaluation research. Each of the steps listed in Chapter 3 requires adequate time.

- Budget enough money (as discussed in the next section). As a general principle, it is important to provide adequate financial resources to fulfill the goals you have for the evaluation, including the reporting and dissemination of the results.

- Develop clear and reasonable standards for communication and progress reports. Specify how you would like to communicate with the evaluator,

---

[37] One of the foremost authorities on evaluation, Michael Patton, *Utilization-Focused Evaluation* (Thousand Oaks, CA: Sage, 2008), stresses in his writings and talks the importance of emphasizing "intended uses by intended users."

the content of the communication, and how often you would like updates on progress.

• Realize there will be some ambiguity. No matter what, some degree of imprecision will always exist in this work. Not everything can be neatly tied down, planned, and explained. Results will rarely, if ever, lead to absolutely clear-cut interpretations and recommendations.

What Does Program Evaluation Cost?

Asking how much evaluation costs is a bit like asking "How much does a house cost?" The answer depends upon exactly what you want, where you want it, and when you want it. So, this section offers some principles you can apply as you consider costs.

Evaluation research, as we have seen, can involve:

• Gathering a little bit of information (lower cost) or a lot of information (higher cost).

• Use of existing information (lower cost) or use of new information (higher cost).

• Use of methods capable of measuring only major results (lower cost) or use of detailed, sensitive methods capable of measuring small and unique results (higher cost).

Another consideration is the time period over which you want to amortize costs. For example, what is the cost of purchasing better insulation for your house? If you look only at the cost of the insulation during the year you install it, the expense might seem large. On the other hand, if you examine your heating costs over the next five years, you may find that you save more in heat bills than you paid for the insulation—so the "cost" is actually a "savings"—real money in your pocket. Ways that evaluation research can save you money or increase your revenues appeared in the discussion of the benefits of evaluation in Chapter 1. They include making programs more effective and efficient, improving your ability to obtain grants and contracts, and improving your public image. Each of these benefits directly or indirectly improves your financial prospects or position.

The next few pages contain some observations that might be helpful as you consider the cost of evaluation. You will note that we discuss this topic in terms of the hours of time necessary to accomplish one example of a program evaluation. Based on the region where you are located, along with customary hourly charges by different types of vendors, you can estimate what this example might cost if it described your program.

An example

Let's take a hypothetical example of a project and its cost, and then we can discuss what this example shows us. We will call the fictitious organization "PeopleServ, Inc." It is a nonprofit organization that has received a program evaluation proposal from a nonprofit research organization.

PeopleServ provides employment training and placement services to hard-to-employ individuals. It serves about 1,200 people each year. Board, management, and staff would like a one-time evaluation to understand the effectiveness of the organization's program, and how its services can improve.

PeopleServ wants to answer the following questions:

- What percentage of clients complete the program?

- Do certain types of clients have a better record of completing the program than others do?

- How satisfied are clients with the services they receive?

- What proportion of clients obtain jobs?

- Are certain types of clients more likely than others to obtain jobs?

- What are the wages for the jobs obtained by clients? Are these wages enough to keep them above the poverty level?

- How many clients who get jobs stay in those jobs for at least six months?

To answer these questions to its satisfaction, PeopleServ and its evaluation consultant, with input from an advisory committee, decide that the evaluation requires:

• Organization and tallying of enrollment and participation records.

• Follow-up interviews with two hundred clients when they complete the program and six months after that.

• Follow-up interviews with fifty program "dropouts."

Table 1 describes how much time the evaluation consulting organization might require to complete the work within each of four phases of the project. These figures are conservative, based on the experiences of many organizations in this situation.

Table 1. Time Required for Project

Phase of Work	Some Activities for the Evaluator*	Time Requirements (A "Conservative" Estimate)
Design	• Three meetings with staff, including preparation and travel • One meeting with advisory committee, including preparation and travel • Selection of measurement instruments • Brief review of literature • Drafting and re-drafting of design, with procedures	• Evaluation researcher: 40 hours • Evaluation assistant: 24 hours • Clerical: 10 hours
Data Collection	• Overseeing and implementing procedures • Tracking survey respondents, based on last available information • Conducting interviews • Editing and coding completed interviews • Storing data in database	• Interviewer supervisor: 60 hours • Evaluation assistant: 25 hours • Interviewers: 450 hours • Programmer: 10 hours
Analysis	• Statistical processing of information • Drafting of written report • Meeting with advisory committee	• Evaluation researcher: 32 hours • Evaluation assistant: 26 hours • Clerical: 10 hours
Reporting	• Issuing final report • Presentation to board of directors, including preparation of presentation graphics as requested by executive director • Extra presentation requested by funders	• Evaluation researcher: 20 hours • Evaluation assistant: 10 hours • Clerical: 12 hours

* For purposes of illustration, I have included only some of the activities of the evaluator. There are more, as we saw in Chapter 3.

Table 2 shows the total hours for the staff who will carry out work on an evaluation project that will provide PeopleServ with the information it needs. Whether PeopleServ uses an evaluation vendor for all of the work, or whether it does some of the work on its own, people with the appropriate set of skills will need to spend these hours to get the project completed.

Table 2. Staff Hours on a Hypothetical Project

Staff	Hours on Project
Evaluation Researcher	92
Evaluation Assistant	85
Admin Support	32
Interviewers	450
Interviewer Supervisor	60
Programmer	10
Total	729

Staff costs typically comprise 85 percent or more of the total cost of an evaluation project. You can multiply expected hours by hourly rates for the different positions to estimate the total cost for staff. Then you can add in other costs.

This example can provide a reference point for you. You may envision an evaluation project for your organization that requires more hours or fewer hours. You may be located in a part of the world with higher or lower costs. Because this organization had done no previous evaluation, design time was anticipated to be longer than for an organization with some previous evaluation experience. Nonetheless, the example provides a starting point to help you think about potential hours necessary to carry out an evaluation project in your own situation.

Keep in mind that not all costs depend equally upon the size of the project. Some costs are relatively fixed. For example, it takes as much time to design a survey for fifty people as for five hundred people. It can take as much time to write a report based on a survey of five hundred people as for fifty people. Other costs vary with size; in the same example, follow-up phone calls to fifty people will be far less expensive than follow-up calls to five hundred people.

A "big data" modification

Could data in an existing database offer opportunities for the example provided above? You should definitely consider that.

The hypothetical organization, PeopleServ, provides employment training and placement services to hard-to-employ individuals. Government agencies, such as state departments of labor or employment, typically maintain records on such individuals. These records include payroll and tax information and unemployment claims, for example. In some locales, organizations can request to use these data to follow up on the success their clients had in securing and maintaining employment.

If PeopleServ wanted to use a source such as state agency employment records, they would likely need to provide identification numbers for the clients who participated in their program. The state agency would process the information and give PeopleServ an aggregate report. In other words, the state agency would report the percentage of clients who had employment for specified numbers of months, or the average earnings of the clients. They might sort some of the data by social characteristics of the clients, as long as the agency felt they could maintain the anonymity of the clients.

Most likely, a state agency would not agree to releasing data on individuals, unless program participants signed a release.

How might this affect costs? Table 3 provides an estimate. You will see some striking differences if you compare Tables 2 and 3. Use of the data provided by a state agency significantly reduces the total number of hours required for the project. It eliminates the costs of interviewing. You will also see what declines slightly or remains close to the same. Time spent by evaluation and administrative support professionals will decline by a small amount. That's because the hours necessary for design, analysis, and reporting would probably, in this case, decline only slightly or remain the same, regardless of the source of the data.

The downside of using existing data in this example is that PeopleServ will not obtain information on the satisfaction and perceptions of the participants in their program. If they consider that information necessary, they will need to do a survey of some sort. They could also consider one or more focus groups—which would provide worthwhile feedback but would not comprise a large representative sample that PeopleServ could use to determine if differences in satisfaction exist among different types of participants (e.g., people with different education levels, different skills, or different amounts of experience).

Table 3. Staff Hours on a Hypothetical Project (Using an Existing Database)

Staff	Hours on Project
Evaluation Researcher	75
Evaluation Assistant	70
Admin Support	32
Interviewers	0
Interviewer Supervisor	0
Programmer	10
Total	187

Summary

This chapter has covered practical issues related to staffing and cost. No single answer exists for the question: Who should do the evaluation research? Nor does one simple answer exist for the question: How much will the evaluation cost? Different options have different advantages and disadvantages. Different options have different costs. Different options suit different organizations, depending upon their skills, resources, and preferences. Even within one organization, management might decide to take diverse approaches to the evaluation of various programs.

The next chapter of this book explores ways you can be sure the evaluation you conduct credibly demonstrates whether and how the work that you do creates impacts.

5

How Can We Show We Make a Difference?

One morning, a public radio station announced what they called the results of an "unscientific" poll—58 percent of the people who telephoned that morning agreed with a particular policy that was discussed on the morning radio show. Some listeners, I am certain, accepted this "unscientifically gathered" information as readily as if it had been "scientifically gathered." I was frustrated that a station I admire would "cheat"—that is, that they would create the impression that they could use comments from a group of listeners to assert that they had a valid sampling of public opinion when in fact they did not (but they could always defend themselves through their claim that they had labeled their findings "unscientific").

What exactly separates "scientific information" from other forms of information? What makes information credible and "valid"? What makes the interpretations and conclusions we draw from a study "correct"? Even for the natural sciences, these questions perplex scientists and philosophers.[38] To reflect on the meaning of science, Michael Patton (one of the foremost authorities on program evaluation) points us toward the Nobel Prize–winning physicist, Percy Bridgman.[39]

---

[38] See, for example, A. F. Chalmers, *What Is This Thing Called Science?* (Buckingham, UK: Open University Press, 1999) for a discussion of what makes science science.

[39] See Michael Q. Patton, " A Historical Perspective on the Evolution of Evaluative Thinking." *New Directions for Evaluation* 2018:158: 11–28.

In his *Reflections of a Physicist*, Bridgman contends that no single "scientific method" exists as such.[40] Scientists solve problems, and they use whatever techniques are required to gather information to solve those problems. The results of those techniques must withstand scrutiny. Transparency is important, so that scientific results can be checked by others and accepted as "objective." In other words, scientists don't set out to follow the scientific method; they set out to solve a problem and don't stop until they have collected enough trustworthy information to do so. The same is true of evaluation.

Many evaluation texts state that to show cause and effect you need to set up experimental designs, identify "control groups," and engage in other "scientific procedures." But strategic management judgments about programs and policies are a blend of scientific reasoning, politics, values, and common sense. As a program manager, you do not have the obligation to produce evaluation research findings that meet some abstract criteria of "science." Rather, you need to make sure that your evaluation study is *believable* to people to whom the study matters and can withstand sincere, reasonable challenges. Your task is to make the results of your work *as credible as possible to the greatest number of relevant people.*

So, what exactly does that mean? If you want to show you make a difference, if you want to claim that your program or service produced an important positive change, if you want to reassure yourself, your board, your funders, and your consumers that you are doing the right thing—how can you make sure that your evaluation work includes whatever features it requires to fulfill your needs?

Guidelines for making the results of your work as credible as possible to the greatest number of people appear in Figure 13. Remember, we are just trying to increase the probability that people will accept your findings and conclusions. In a realm that includes politics and values, there are no guarantees that everyone will believe your evaluation.

---

[40] Percy Bridgman, *Reflections of a Physicist*, (New York: Philosophical Library, 1955).

Figure 13. Guidelines for Credible Findings

Guideline	Reason Why It's Important
Show your work.	Many of us heard this frequently from our mathematics teachers. It pertains to evaluation research as well. If people can see the methods you used and can examine data on their own, they can assess what you did and feel confident about your conclusions. Some evaluation studies do not afford this opportunity to their readers, and the credibility of these studies suffers as a result.
Include the four essential types of evaluation information: client information, service data, documentation of results, and perception data (see these types of information described in Chapter 2).	If you have this information, you will be in a very strong position to provide a portrait of what you are doing and to respond to any questions or concerns people may have about your findings.
Match your method to your conclusions.	If you are at an early stage of exploring how your program is working, it's fine to talk to an easily-assembled number of participants (a "convenience sample") to get some preliminary feedback. Or, if you just want to obtain suggestions for potential improvements of the program, it's fine to schedule some focus groups for whoever can show up. The resulting information can be very meaningful, and it can lead to productive changes.

On the other hand, if you want to confirm that you are effective and making a difference with your programs, you'll need to draw a more representative sample over a sufficient period of time. You'll need to measure things in such a way that both you and other readers of the evaluation findings can count numbers and see improvements. So, for example, if you and others are concerned about barriers that keep people from obtaining your service, it would be reasonable to remain skeptical of any findings that only included the opinions of people who come in your door. You need to talk with people who can't get there or people who have dropped out. |

Figure 13. Guidelines for Credible Findings (continued)

Guideline	Reason Why It's Important
Include some sort of program theory.	People accept cause and effect conclusions more readily if the conclusions fit within a reasonable framework that lets everyone know why things happen the way they do. The discussion of program theories in Chapter 2 showed that techniques such as logic models can provide coherence and context that strengthen the credibility of findings.
Include enough participants in your study.	A case study of one person who receives services from your program can be very enlightening and worthwhile. Unfortunately, it won't provide convincing evidence that your service is effective. It also does not allow you to identify any differences that might exist among different types of people who come to your program. Larger numbers increase the confidence of people who want to use evaluation results to shape programs and policies and to make funding decisions. Conclusions from a study with 250 participants will, on average, seem more solid than conclusions from a study with 25 participants.
Have a comparison.	The strongest evidence of cause and effect is a good comparison. Because of its importance, we will discuss it in detail in the next section.

We have touched on most of these guidelines already, in Chapter 2. One of them—having a "comparison"—is something we have not discussed. We will spend some time on it here.

CASE EXAMPLE:
Using Comparison Data

What's the study?

Behavioral Health Homes program evaluation

Topic of study:

Behavioral health, health care

What were the evaluation study questions?

To learn...

- What are the successes of the Behavioral Health Homes model so far?
- What challenges are service sites encountering in implementing Behavioral Health Homes services?

Methods used:

Interviews with recipients and providers, analysis of health care claims data

How was it done?

Wilder Research developed interview protocols for service recipients and providers, with assistance from the Minnesota Department of Human Services (DHS) and the Minnesota chapter of the National Alliance on Mental Illness (NAMI-MN). Then the researchers and NAMI-MN conducted phone interviews with recipients and providers.

Wilder Research also analyzed health care claims data from DHS to examine outcomes for service recipients. Using these health care claims data, the researchers created a comparison group of claims filers who were eligible for Behavioral Health Homes services but were not receiving services. This comparison group allowed the researchers to compare outcomes between services recipients and a similar group of people who had not received services. Claims data provided information on health care use (e.g., average length of inpatient hospitalizations, access to preventive care, average number of mental health services received), alcohol and drug treatment initiation and engagement, and health care costs.

What's the takeaway?

There are multiple ways to include comparison data in your evaluation. In this case, the data collected by DHS as part of their claims process presented a ready comparison group for the evaluation. If you work with or receive funding from government agencies, you could explore getting comparison data from them for evaluation purposes. In other cases, you may have to gather your own comparison data, for example by identifying people who are similar to those you serve and then surveying them in addition to surveying your program participants.

Developing a credible comparison

Presumably, you expect that your program will produce some positive outcomes. Let's say that 80 percent of the participants in your program do, in fact, achieve those outcomes. Can you claim that your service benefits four out of five people receiving it and that your service helped them to achieve the desired outcomes? Most program managers have the experience to know that you cannot make that claim. It's quite possible that 80 percent of the participants might have achieved those outcomes anyway, without any help from your program. Possession of information based solely on people who received your service does not provide you with the strongest possible evidence of program impacts.

For this reason, many evaluation practitioners would state that you need a *control group*. A control group is a group of people who qualify for your service, but they are randomly assigned not to receive the service. This allows you to observe how they differ over time from those who are randomly assigned to receive the service. For some studies, control groups are very valuable, even necessary. For most evaluation research, however, control groups are not practical.

Remember, your task is to make the results of your work *as credible as possible to the greatest number of relevant people*. You need to identify some form of comparison that will supply sufficiently compelling evidence to the people who are the primary stakeholders or users of your study. In most cases, this will not require the inclusion of a control group in your evaluation research.

What sort of comparisons will strengthen your study and make it as credible as possible to the greatest number of people? In studies of programs that attempt to achieve outcomes with individuals or families, five types of comparison are credible. These are comparing service recipients to themselves over time, comparing them to people waiting for service, comparing them to similar people in the general population, comparing them to a control group as described above, and comparing them to people in similar programs. These comparisons are described in Figure 14.

Sometimes, programs focus on whole communities. They want to show that their activities had impacts at a community level. The principles for

making comparisons to demonstrate the impact of individual-serving programs also apply to programs that focus on communities. When evaluating community outcomes, you will use community indicators—employment rate, school readiness level, poverty level, housing vacancies, or whatever is appropriate—to monitor whether conditions improve, stay the same, or worsen before and after you do your work.

Figure 14. Credible Comparisons for Program Evaluations

Comparison	Value
Comparing service recipients to themselves over time	This is the weakest form of comparison, but it's still better than nothing. It requires taking an initial measure to establish a baseline and then taking one or more measurements later, either while they are receiving your service or immediately after their participation in the program. This procedure offers the opportunity to provide evidence that the people's situation improved or that they had their needs met. This can support the supposition that such improvement might have occurred because of your program. Moreover, if you can't detect any improvement, you have obtained some very important information that the service might not produce intended outcomes.
	This comparison approach is often called "pre-post" because you measure before the program (pre) and then again after the program (post) and compare the results.
	For a community-level intervention: This comparison involves looking over time at the community(ies) that received your program's services.
Comparing service recipients to people waiting for service	Often, people have applied to take part in a program and have essentially identical needs and characteristics to those who participate in the program, but space doesn't allow the program to fit them in. These people can be a handy source of comparative information. If you can gather this information over a long enough time period, they become a reasonable comparison group to provide some evidence of the effectiveness of your program. (However, since you want to bring them into the program, it might not be possible to gather enough comparative information before you initiate service delivery to them.)
	For a community-level intervention: Sometimes, many communities apply to be part of a program, but not all can start at the same time, or some are told to reapply at a later time. You can compare communities that participate right away with those on the waiting list.

Figure 14. Credible Comparisons for Program Evaluations (continued)

Comparison	Value
Comparing service recipients to similar individuals in the general population	Your community may have many people who could benefit from your service but who do not receive it. If you can contact them to obtain information, and if they don't differ from service recipients in any way that would call your analysis into question, then they may serve as a good comparison group. For a community-level intervention: You can compare communities on which your program focuses with communities that do not receive your services. It is important to select comparison communities that resemble your community as closely as possible on important demographics such as age, race, income, etc. Also, they should have some similarity with respect to the issue or need that you address.
Comparing service-eligible people who are randomly assigned to the service group or the no-service group	This is the traditional control group in an experimental design. It is sometimes called a Randomized Controlled Trial (RCT). In the language of experimentalists, if you make this comparison, any differences you identify between service recipients and non-recipients have resulted only from (a) your impact and (b) chance fluctuations. If you feel confident that chance fluctuations remain at a minimum, then better results in the service group provide strong evidence that your program has made a positive difference. For a community-level intervention: If you can serve multiple communities, then you could randomly assign some communities to receive your services and others not to receive your services. You could then compare the two groups.

References

Adams, Adrienne E., Nkiru A. Nnawulezi, and Lela Vandenberg. 2015. "'Expectations to Change' (E2C): A Participatory Method for Facilitating Stakeholder Engagement with Evaluation Findings." *American Journal of Evaluation* 36(2): 243–255.

AISP. 2020. *Centering Data Equity Throughout Data Integration*. Philadelphia: University of Pennsylvania.

Altschuld, James W. 1999. "The Certification of Evaluators: Highlights from a Report Submitted to the Board of Directors of the American Evaluation Association." *American Journal of Evaluation* 20: 481–493.

Bickman, Leonard, and Debra J. Rog. 2009. *Handbook of Applied Social Research Methods*. Thousand Oaks, California: Sage.

Bridgman, Percy W. 1955. *Reflections of a Physicist*. New York: Philosophical Library.

Bryan, Michelle, and Ashlee Lewis. 2019. "Culturally Responsive Evaluation as a Form of Critical Qualitative Inquiry." *Oxford Research Encyclopedias* https://oxfordre.com/education/view/10.1093/acrefore/9780190264093.001.0001/acrefore-9780190264093-e-545

Caracelli, Valerie J., and Hallie Preskill. 2000. *The Expanding Scope of Evaluation Use*. San Francisco: Jossey-Bass.

Centers for Disease Control and Prevention. 2013. *Evaluation Reporting: A Guide to Help Ensure Use of Evaluation Findings*. Atlanta, Georgia: US Department of Health and Human Services.

Chalmers, A.F. 1999. *What Is This Thing Called Science?* Buckingham, United Kingdom: Open University Press.

Cook, James R. 2014. "Using Evaluation to Effect Social Change: Looking Through a Community Psychology Lens." *American Journal of Evaluation* 36(1): 107–117.

Davies, Randall, Dan Randall, and Richard E. West. 2015. "Using Open Badges to Certify Practicing Evaluators." *American Journal of Evaluation* 36(2): 151–163.

Fierro, Leslie A., and Christina A. Christie. 2017. "Evaluator and Program Manager Perceptions of Evaluation Capacity and Evaluation Practice." *American Journal of Evaluation* 38(3): 376–392.

Hosley, Cheryl. 2000. *Strategies for Measuring Accessibility of Mental Health Programs*. Saint Paul: Amherst H. Wilder Foundation.

Inkelas, Moira, Patricia Bowie, and Lila Guirguis. 2017. "Improvement for a Community Population: The Magnolia Community Initiative." *New Directions for Program Evaluation* 153: 51–64.

Iwaniec, Dorothy, and John Pinkerton. 1998. *Making Research Work*. Chichester, England: John Wiley & Sons.

Jones, Steven C., and Blaine R. Worthen. 1999. "AEA Members' Opinions Concerning Evaluator Certification." *American Journal of Evaluation* 20: 495–506.

King, Jean A. (ed.). 2020. "The American Evaluation Association's Program Evaluator Competencies." *New Directions for Evaluation* 168.

Levi-Strauss, Claude. 1966. *The Savage Mind*. Chicago: University of Chicago Press.

Mattessich, Paul W. 2001. "Lessons Learned: What These Seven Studies Teach Us." *Cancer Practice* 9: 78–84.

Mattessich, Paul W. 2012. "Advisory Committees in Contract and Grant-Funded Research." *New Directions for Evaluation* 136: 31–48.

Mattessich, Paul W., and Barbara R. Monsey. 1998. *Stating Outcomes for American Cancer Society Programs*. Atlanta: American Cancer Society.

Mattessich, Paul W., and Kirsten M. Johnson. 2018. *Collaboration: What Makes It Work* (3rd edition). Nashville: Turner Publishing Company.

Mattessich, Paul W., Daniel Mueller, and Cheryl Holm-Hansen. 2009. "Managing Evaluation for Program Improvement at the Wilder Foundation." *New Directions for Evaluation* 121: 27–42.

Mattessich, Paul W., Donald W. Compton, and Michael Baizerman. 2001. "Evaluation Use and the Collaborative Evaluation Fellows Project." *Cancer Practice* 9: 85–91.

Mattessich, Paul W., Marta Murray-Close, and Barbara R. Monsey. 2001. *Collaboration: What Makes It Work* (2nd edition). Saint Paul, MN: Amherst H. Wilder Foundation.

Maxwell, Nan L., Dana Rotz, and Christina Garcia. 2016. "Data and Decision Making: Same Organization, Different Perceptions; Different Organizations, Different Perceptions." *American Journal of Evaluation* 37(4): 463–485.

Measuring Program Outcomes: A Practical Approach. 1996. Alexandria, Virginia: United Way of America.

Patton, Michael Quinn. 2008. *Utilization-Focused Evaluation*. Thousand Oaks, California: Sage.

Patton, Michael Quinn. 2018. "A Historical Perspective on the Evolution of Evaluative Thinking." *New Directions for Evaluation* 158: 11–28.

Pecora, Peter J., Mark W. Fraser, Kristine E. Nelson, Jacquelyn McCroskey, and William Meezan. 1995. *Evaluating Family-Based Services*. New York: Aldine De Gruyter.

Picciotto, Robert. 2020. "Evaluation and the Big Data Challenge." *American Journal of Evaluation*. 41(2): 166–181.

Price, Ann Webb, Kyrah K. Brown, and Susan M. Wolfe. 2020. "What Are Coalitions and Collaboratives?" *New Directions for Program Evaluation* 165: 9–16.

Pritchett, Rachel, Jeremy Kemp, Philip Wilson, Helen Minnis, Graham Bryce, and Christopher Gillberg. 2011. "Quick, simple measures of family relationships for use in clinical practice and research. A systematic review." *Family Practice* 28(2): 172–187.

Ralser, Tom. 2007. *ROI for Nonprofits*. Hoboken, NJ: John Wiley & Sons.

Rogers, Patricia J., Anthony Petrosino, Tracy A. Huebner, and Timothy A. Hacsi. 2000. "Program Theory Evaluation: Practice, Promise, and Problems." In *Program Theory in Evaluation: Challenges and Opportunities*, edited by Patricia J. Rogers, Timothy A. Hacsi, Anthony Petrosino, and Tracy A. Huebner, 5–13. San Francisco: Jossey-Bass.

Shakespeare, William. *As You Like It*. Edited by Alan Brissenden. Oxford: Oxford University Press, 1993.

Thomas, Veronica, Henry Frierson, Stafford Hood, and Gerunda Hughes. 2010. "A Guide to Conducting Culturally Responsive Evaluations." In Joy Frechtling, *The 2010 User-Friendly Handbook for Program Evaluation*, 75–96. 2010. Washington, DC: National Science Foundation.

Index